In the Kitchen
with Rosie

In the Kitchen with
Rosie

Oprah's Favorite Recipes

by Rosie Daley

Alfred A. Knopf   NEW YORK   *1994*

THIS IS A BORZOI BOOK,
PUBLISHED BY ALFRED A. KNOPF, INC.

Copyright © 1994 by Rosie Daley
All rights reserved under International and Pan-American
Copyright Conventions. Published in the United States by
Alfred A. Knopf, Inc., New York, and simultaneously in Canada
by Random House of Canada Limited, Toronto. Distributed by
Random House, Inc., New York.

ISBN 0-679-43404-6

Manufactured in the United States of America
Published May 1, 1994
Reprinted Thirteen Times
Fifteenth Printing, June 1994

Dedicated to OPRAH *and* STEDMAN,

*for the opportunity to create healthy food and share it
with everyone who reads this book,
for letting me be me, and for the pleasure of working
for such wonderful people*

Contents

Acknowledgments

Special thanks to Barry Bluestein and Kevin Morrissey for the time they spent organizing and rewriting my recipes—making this book possible.

Thanks also to Fabio Marchi, Kris Walters, Jeff Hauptman, Debrah Fonda Carl, Mrs. Eddins, and the Cal-a-Vie Health Spa for inspiration on some dishes, and to Marley St. John and all my friends who encouraged me and had faith in my talent and skills.

Introduction

Some of my fondest early memories are of my grandmother over a stove fixin' food for our daily feast.

I grew up eating well. Cheese grits, homemade biscuits smothered in butter, home-cured ham, red-eyed gravy—and that was just breakfast. Smothered chicken, butter beans, fried corn, and corn bread was a typical weekday dinner. Sunday supper (when the preacher from the church down the road would often stop by) was a celebration. Food was the guest of honor, covering so much of the table there was hardly room for plates.

Back then food meant security and comfort. Food meant love. It didn't matter what you ate, just that you had enough. I've paid a heavy price for believing that. It took me a long time to change the way I thought about food.

I once believed that eating healthy meant eating food that was missing something—TASTE. I once believed eating healthy meant being unsatisfied. I once believed eating healthy meant no security, no comfort, no love.

Several years ago while visiting yet another spa, trying one more time to jump-start myself into health and fitness, I sat down for the orientation lunch and had a meal so delicious I thought it couldn't possibly be spa food. I asked immediately, who cooked this and how did they do it? How can this possibly be less than 300 calories?

After every meal I would go into the kitchen and talk to the chef. Her name was Rosie. I begged her to come home and cook for me. Six months later, she moved to Chicago and changed the way I thought about food forever.

This new way of eating very low fat, low sugar, low salt (I like to call it "clean eating") has made such a difference in my life. I feel better. But do not be misled: changing the way you think about food is only the first step toward achieving and maintaining a desirable weight. It was only through a comprehensive plan of healthy eating, daily exercise, and changing my self-defeating behavior that I was able to release weight as an issue from my life.

Real cooking is an art form. A gift to be shared. I've had some fabulous meals from Rosie's kitchen, but the recipes in this book are my all-time favorites. The ones I ask her to cook again and again.

Oprah Winfrey

In the Kitchen
with Rosie

Cooking Notes from Chef Rosie

*F*ood is a necessity; preparing it is an art. I love to create, and cooking gives me a wonderful opportunity to do so.

This book includes basic techniques and simple recipes for preparing food that is nutritious, filling, and light in fat but far from bland. Cooking healthy meals can be challenging, but it's just as satisfying and self-fulfilling as preparing rich dishes. Like anything else you want to have turn out well, it takes energy, devotion, love, and a desire to create.

I try to appeal to the stomach through the visual. Your whole body is present at the table—and the prettier the plate, the more enjoyable the experience.

Garnishing a dish leaves considerable room for expression, for working with pattern and color. I apply my design skills to create plates that are as satisfying to the eye as to the palate, using orange-slice wheels, scallion starbursts, or pretty radish rosettes. There are a lot of specialized garnishing tools available, but you can create the most beautiful food with just a knife and a little imagination.

Let your plate be your canvas. Be aware of colors and how they accent each other. A simple tomato slice placed on the salad in a unique way can catch the eye.

Put your personal touch on my recipes. As you cook the dish, it becomes your work of art to share. Let love flow through your cooking—a gift for yourself and for others.

Ingredients and Techniques

First, organize your kitchen and familiarize yourself with it. Be comfortable and expect the best. Read recipes all the way through before starting; it's helpful to have all the ingredients and utensils you'll need handy.

Enjoy all aspects of creating good food, from shopping to chopping. Start with the freshest of ingredients and your end product will reflect the quality. Handpick what you eat and be selective. Always rinse meat, fish, and produce thoroughly.

Good fruits and vegetables are a passion of mine. For the sweetest and the tartest, choose produce in season—look for what's plentiful.

I use fresh vegetable purees as the basis for thick and rich "cream" soups, dispensing with cream and butter without compromising flavor. Freshly squeezed lemon, lime, or orange juice is a must in most of my salad dressings; and I use small amounts of citrus zest to enhance the flavor of baked goods and sauces.

Fruit juices make wonderful marinades, bringing out the maximum flavor of poultry and fish. Like honey and maple syrup, fruit juices are natural sweeteners that can easily replace sugar.

Fresh herbs, which most supermarkets carry in the produce section, will accent the natural flavor of whatever you serve. Whole leaves of basil, chervil, cilantro, and mint are usually a part of my salad greens. Often, I cook with dried herbs and save the fresh herbs for garnish so that their full flavor can be savored. When using dried herbs, remember that they are much stronger than fresh; use only ¼ to ⅓ as much.

Small amounts of toasted nuts and seeds add texture and protein to salads. They're very flavorful, and although they do contain fat, a little of the nuts or seeds goes a long way.

Vinegars add life, but no fat and virtually no calories, to a range of dishes. If you look in your supermarket, you'll see that they now come in a multitude of flavors and hues. I particularly like raspberry, balsamic, red wine, and tarragon vinegars.

Several of my recipes call for plain nonfat yogurt. It adds moisture to baked goods and is a good substitute for mayonnaise in salads and dressings.

I substitute skim milk, 2% milk, and evaporated skim milk for cream and whole milk, using a little flour or cornstarch to thicken if needed.

When buying packaged and canned goods, always read labels carefully. Compare brands and choose those lowest in fat and calories. The calorie and fat counts for my recipes are based upon the lowest-fat and lowest-calorie products readily available.

Soups

*L*ong *before* I started to love soup, I loved the idea of it. As a girl I watched "Lassie" every Sunday night. At the end of the show was a Campbell's commercial. Timmy's mom would feed him m'm-m'm-good soup. I believed the soup could warm my tummy and my heart. Just like the announcer said.

Soup and sandwich—well, there could be nothing better. I wanted my mom to give me soup and sandwich just like Timmy's mom did.

Soup and sandwich—it's still my favorite thing to have for lunch. I have it almost every day in winter, and in the summer I have soup and salad. It always leaves me feeling warm and satisfied.

Oprah

Black Bean and Smoked Chicken Soup

*H*ealthy black beans, or turtle beans, are a terrific source of protein and carbohydrates. In this recipe, inspired by George's Restaurant in La Jolla, California, the smoky flavor characteristic of black bean soup is intensified by liquid smoke and chicken baked with barbecue sauce, rather than from the usual bacon or ham. Look for the liquid smoke in the spice section of your market.

½ cup dried black beans
2 cups water
1 bay leaf
Light vegetable oil cooking spray
½ cup peeled and chopped broccoli stems
½ cup scraped and cubed carrot (1 medium carrot)
1 cup scraped and cubed celery (2 medium stalks)
1 cup chopped onion (1 medium onion)
1 tablespoon dried thyme
1 tablespoon dried basil
½ cup dry white wine
8 ounces boneless, skinless chicken breast
4 tablespoons barbecue sauce (no-oil variety)
1 cup chicken stock, fat skimmed off
12 ounces evaporated skim milk
2 cups broccoli florets (1 bundle)

(continued on page 10)

Serves 4

Fat per serving =
  3.6 grams
Calories per serving = 368

(Black Bean and Smoked Chicken Soup, continued)

1 tablespoon cornstarch dissolved in 2 table
   spoons cold water
1 tablespoon liquid smoke
1 tablespoon Worcestershire sauce
1 teaspoon Tabasco sauce
¼ cup chopped fresh cilantro

Pick over and rinse the beans. Put them into a large bowl and cover completely with cold water. Let the beans soak overnight (or for at least 8 hours).

Drain the beans and transfer them to a medium saucepan. Add the 2 cups water and the bay leaf. Bring to a boil over medium heat and cook for 15 minutes. Reduce the heat to low and simmer, uncovered, for about 20 minutes, until the beans are tender. Drain the beans and discard the bay leaf.

Preheat the oven to 400 degrees.

Place a heavy stockpot over medium heat for about 1 minute, then spray it twice with the vegetable oil. Add the broccoli stems, carrot, celery, and onion. Cover, reduce the heat to low, and cook for 5 minutes, stirring once or twice. Stir in the thyme, basil, and wine. Simmer, uncovered, for about 15 minutes, until the wine has been reduced by half.

In the meantime, coat the chicken thoroughly with the barbecue sauce and bake for 10 minutes on the top shelf of the oven. Remove the chicken from the oven and allow it to cool just long enough to handle. Cut the chicken into small cubes.

Add the chicken, chicken stock, and beans to the stockpot. Cook over low heat for about 3 minutes, until thoroughly heated. Stir in the evaporated milk and the broccoli florets. Cook for 5 minutes, stirring if needed to keep the soup from coming to a boil. Add the dissolved cornstarch and cook for 2 minutes more, stirring constantly. Stir in the liquid smoke, Worcestershire sauce, and Tabasco sauce.

Garnish with the chopped cilantro.

Soaking Dried Beans

I think overnight soaking makes for the best beans—plump and tender—but you can use this alternative method to save time. Put the beans into a saucepan large enough to accommodate a volume of water four times that of the beans. Bring to a boil over high heat and boil for 5 minutes. Cover the pan, remove it from the heat, and let the beans sit for 1 hour. Drain before proceeding to the next step of cooking the beans.

In a pinch, you can use canned beans—no soaking necessary. But be sure to rinse and drain the beans thoroughly.

Corn Chowder

I make this "creamy" corn chowder without any cream! The pureed corn lends the soup its thick, silky texture. Use fresh corn in season; substitute frozen corn only when fresh isn't available.

Serves 4

*Fat per serving =
3.1 grams*
Calories per serving = 229

Light vegetable oil cooking spray
1 cup chopped onion (1 medium onion)
6 cups fresh corn kernels (12 ears), with any milk collected when removed from the cob
3 cups chicken stock, fat skimmed off
½ cup chopped red bell pepper
½ teaspoon chopped fresh rosemary
½ teaspoon dried thyme
⅛ teaspoon freshly ground black pepper
Cayenne pepper to taste
1 tablespoon chopped fresh basil

Preheat a large, heavy saucepan over medium heat for about 1 minute. Spray it twice with the vegetable oil. Sauté the onion for about 5 minutes, until translucent. Add 4 cups of the corn and sauté for 4 to 5 minutes, until it softens a bit. Add 2 cups of the chicken stock and cook until the corn can be mashed easily with a fork, about 20 minutes.

Transfer the contents of the pan to a blender and puree until smooth. Return the puree to the saucepan over medium-low heat. Add the bell pepper, rosemary, thyme, black pepper, cayenne pepper, and the remaining 1 cup chicken stock and 2 cups corn. Stir and cook for about 10 minutes more, until the chowder is thick and creamy.

Garnish with the chopped basil.

Removing Corn Kernels from the Cob

Remove the husk and silk from an ear of corn. Hold it vertically over a plate positioned to collect the kernels and the milk that will spurt when the kernels are removed from the cob. Scrape down the cob with a sharp knife, releasing the kernels. Rotate the cob and repeat until all kernels have been removed.

The process is even easier with the aid of a handy gadget, available from many kitchenware stores, that frees all the kernels in one motion. Fitted with a saw-toothed circle that slips over the tip of the corn, the apparatus is simply pushed down the length of the ear, releasing the kernels.

Cream of Broccoli Soup

*B*ecause I use low-fat evaporated skim milk instead of heavy cream, this velvety soup has only 1½ grams of fat per serving. Adding the bouillon cube to the water in which the broccoli cooks lends added richness; if you're on a limited-salt diet, use a reduced-sodium bouillon cube.

Serves 4

Fat per serving = 1.5 grams
Calories per serving = 211

½ cup water
1 chicken bouillon cube
3 cups broccoli florets and peeled stems (1 large bundle)
24 ounces evaporated skim milk
Light vegetable oil cooking spray
1½ cups chopped leek, white part only (2–3 leeks)
2 tablespoons all-purpose flour
½ teaspoon ground nutmeg
1 garlic clove, peeled and minced
3 tablespoons chopped fresh basil
Freshly ground black pepper to taste

Bring the water to a boil in a medium saucepan over medium heat. Dissolve the bouillon cube in the boiling water. Add the broccoli and cook for 5 to 6 minutes, until it is bright green and fork tender.

Put the evaporated milk in a small saucepan. Warm over low heat, just until bubbles begin to form around the edge. Remove the pan from the heat.

Preheat a large, heavy saucepan over medium heat for about 1 minute. Spray it twice with the vegetable oil. Add the leeks and sauté, stirring often, for 7 to 8 minutes, until limp. Stir in the flour and cook for 1 minute. Whisk in the warm evaporated milk. Continue to cook, whisking constantly, until the flour has dissolved and the mixture is smooth.

Reduce the heat to low. Add the nutmeg, the garlic, and the broccoli, along with its cooking liquid. Simmer for 5 minutes more, taking care not to bring the soup to a boil. Remove the pan from the heat and stir in the basil and black pepper.

Vegetable Barley Stew with Lentils

A meal in itself, this substantial soup really takes the chill off Chicago winters. Sometimes I add a dash of hot sauce or a little Parmesan cheese.

For company, I garnish the stew with carrot flowers.

Serves 6

Fat per serving = 1.5 grams
Calories per serving = 316

1 cup pearl barley
6 cups water
Light vegetable oil cooking spray
1 cup chopped onion (1 medium onion)
1½ cups scraped and chopped carrot (2–3 carrots)
1 cup dried lentils
1 bay leaf
½ teaspoon grated fresh ginger
1 tablespoon dried basil
1 tablespoon dried thyme
1 tablespoon dried oregano
3 cups low-sodium V8 juice
1 cup chopped zucchini (1 small zucchini)
1 cup chopped red bell pepper (1 medium pepper)
1 tablespoon chopped jalapeño pepper (1 small pepper)
1 cup scraped and chopped celery (2 medium stalks)
1 cup chopped tomato (1 medium tomato)
2 cups chopped mushrooms
6 garlic cloves, peeled and minced

2 tablespoons reduced-sodium soy sauce
½ cup chopped fresh parsley

Combine the barley and 4 cups of water in a medium saucepan. Bring to a boil over medium heat and cook for 5 minutes. Reduce the heat to low and simmer for 30 minutes, then remove the pan from the heat.

Put a heavy stockpot over medium heat for about 1 minute. Spray it twice with the vegetable oil. Add the onion and carrots. Sauté, stirring constantly, for 3 minutes. Stir in the lentils, bay leaf, ginger, dried herbs, and remaining 2 cups water. Bring the mixture to a boil, cover, and reduce the heat to low. Simmer for about 20 minutes, until the lentils are tender.

Add the V8 juice, zucchini, peppers, celery, and tomato to the pot. Cook over low heat until the vegetables are tender, about 10 minutes. Pour in the barley and its cooking liquid. Stir in the mushrooms, garlic, and soy sauce. Cook for 10 minutes more to thicken the stew.

Garnish with the chopped parsley.

Making Carrot Flowers

With the tip of a vegetable scraper, carve 4 equally spaced gullies into the surface of a peeled carrot lengthwise. Cut the carrot into ¼-inch slices and scatter them over the stew after ladling it into soup bowls.

Curried Mushroom Soup

*T*his soup is tangy in its mildest rendition, and just gets hotter, depending on the strength of the curry used. For added tastebud tingling, dust with cayenne pepper.

Today one can find a variety of marvelous wild mushrooms, even in the supermarket. Use what is available. For the dried mushrooms, I like the mix of oyster, morel, and porcini, but a cup of any single variety can be substituted. Garnish with chopped parsley if you can't find chervil.

Serves 4

Fat per serving = 1.6 grams
Calories per serving = 196

2 cups boiling water
1 cup assorted dried oyster, morel, and porcini mushrooms (1 ounce dried mushrooms)
Light vegetable oil cooking spray
1½ cups chopped leek, white part only (2–3 leeks)
2 tablespoons all-purpose flour
1 tablespoon curry powder (see Box, page 36)
4 cups skim milk
1 chicken bouillon cube
2 cups chopped fresh portobello mushrooms (3 smallish mushrooms)
4 cups chopped fresh shiitake mushrooms (10–12 mushrooms)
1 tablespoon dry sherry
1 tablespoon chopped fresh chervil

Curried Mushroom Soup with a Grilled Vegetable Sandwich
(a Pizza Dough Baguette fresh from the oven in the background)

Rosie tossing her Spinach Salad in Fresh Orange Dressing with Pine Nuts

Pour the boiling water over the dried mushrooms in a bowl and set aside to soak.

Preheat a heavy stockpot over medium heat for about 1 minute, then spray it twice with the vegetable oil. Add the leeks and sauté for about 3 minutes, stirring constantly, until translucent. Add the flour and curry powder. Stir with a wooden spoon until the leeks are well coated. Add the milk and bouillon cube. Raise the heat to high and cook just until bubbles begin to form around the edge.

Reduce the heat to low and whisk until all ingredients are thoroughly combined. Stir in the fresh mushrooms and cook for 5 minutes.

Meanwhile, remove the reconstituted mushrooms from their soaking liquid, strain, squeeze out excess moisture, and roughly chop. (Save the soaking liquid for another soup or sauce; here it would thin the soup too much and curdle the skim milk.) Add to the stockpot and cook for 1 minute more. Stir in the sherry.

Garnish with the chopped chervil.

Cauliflower Puree with Peas

*T*his deceptively mild soup is actually brimming with flavorful seasonings. The vitamin- and protein-rich brown rice miso, a soybean paste, is stocked in the ethnic section of larger markets and by Asian groceries. Spike seasoning is an herb mix that can be found on your supermarket's spice rack.

You can create a variety of robust, healthy vegetable purees using this recipe. Try substituting an equal amount of trimmed and chopped asparagus, carrot, or spinach for the cauliflower.

Serves 4

Fat per serving = 0.5 grams
Calories per serving = 98

5 cups cauliflower florets (1 head)
3 cups vegetable stock
1 tablespoon brown rice miso
1 tablespoon low-fat cream cheese
1 tablespoon Spike seasoning
¼ cup scraped and finely cubed carrot
¼ cup scraped and finely cubed celery
¼ cup chopped scallion, white part only (2–3 scallions)
1 teaspoon Louisiana-style hot sauce
¼ teaspoon ground white pepper
½ cup fresh peas or frozen peas, thawed

Combine the cauliflower and vegetable stock in a stockpot. Cook over medium heat for about 20 minutes, until the cauliflower is fork tender.

Transfer the contents of the pot to a blender, add the miso and cream cheese, and puree until smooth. Return the puree to the stockpot. Add all remaining ingredients except the peas and cook over low heat for about 5 minutes, until the vegetables are tender. Stir in the peas.

Watch Out for the Sand in Dried Mushrooms

Many varieties of dried wild mushrooms harbor a lot of residual sand, which accumulates in the bottom of the soaking bowl when the mushrooms are reconstituted. If you then pour the contents of the bowl into a strainer, the sand can easily be reabsorbed into the mushrooms. Instead, lift each mushroom from the soaking liquid individually and transfer it to the strainer, taking care not to dislodge sand from the bottom of the bowl.

Salads

I *never cared* much for salads. But what I really disliked was boring salads. Now I know a salad can be as good as your imagination. Forget iceberg! Think Boston, chicory, radicchio, arugula, endive.

Experiment! Use any combination of your favorite greens and add the dressing of your palate's desire. Delicious!

Oprah

Grilled Chicken Salad

*M*arinate the chicken in the seasoned lemon juice, soy sauce, and garlic mixture for up to 2 hours; the longer it marinates, the more flavorful and tender the chicken. For variety, I substitute an equal amount of lime or grapefruit juice for the lemon juice in the marinade.

For a special visual treat, garnish each serving of salad with a radish rosette.

5 tablespoons freshly squeezed lemon juice
3 tablespoons reduced-sodium soy sauce
2 garlic cloves, peeled and chopped
⅛ teaspoon freshly ground black pepper
1 teaspoon dried basil
8 ounces boneless, skinless chicken breast
1 large red onion, trimmed and cut into ⅛-inch rounds
Light vegetable oil cooking spray
1 pound mixed salad greens (6 cups)
1 tablespoon crumbled blue cheese
1 medium tomato, cored and cut into 8 wedges

FOR THE DRESSING

4 tablespoons freshly squeezed lemon juice
4 tablespoons balsamic vinegar
2 garlic cloves, peeled
2 teaspoons dried basil

Serves 4

*Fat per serving =
3.2 grams
Calories per serving = 176*

(continued on page 26)

(Grilled Chicken Salad, continued)

Whisk together thoroughly the lemon juice, soy sauce, garlic, black pepper, and basil in a large bowl and set aside.

Place the chicken on a sheet of plastic wrap spread on a work surface and cover it with a second sheet. Pound gently with a mallet. Lift the top sheet of plastic, flip the pieces of chicken over, and re-cover. Evenly pound the second side to a thickness of ¼ inch. Transfer the chicken to the marinade bowl and cover. Marinate in the refrigerator for at least 30 minutes.

Preheat the grill or broiler.

Place the onion rounds in a single layer on a baking sheet and spray lightly with the vegetable oil; turn them over and spray to coat the other side. Remove the chicken from the marinade and place alongside the onion rings. Grill or broil the onion rounds and the chicken for 5 minutes per side. Let the chicken cool a bit, then slice thinly.

Spread an even amount of the mixed greens on 4 salad plates, scatter the onion rounds and then the sliced chicken on top. Sprinkle ¾ teaspoon blue cheese over each. Garnish with the tomato wedges.

Making a Radish Rosette

Trim the root end of each radish and slice about ⅛ inch squarely off the top. Cut a cross into the radish, slicing about ⅔ of the way down from the top. Turn the radish about 45 degrees and cut another cross to create 8 equal segments. Cover the radishes with ice water and soak for about 15 minutes, until the rosettes fan open.

Combine all the dressing ingredients in a blender and mix at low speed until the garlic is finely chopped. Spoon dressing onto the salads or serve it on the side.

Stovetop Grilling

A variety of stovetop fixtures are now available that bring the flavor of outdoor grilling right into the kitchen year-round.

The classic cast-iron block stands on low legs over the burner. It has a corrugated surface that leaves grill marks on the food and is angled slightly so that fat runs down into a gutter. This type of grill is a little cumbersome, but works the best.

A second variety, which sits level on the burner, has a corrugated surface on one side and a flat griddle on the other. Many of these grills have handles and can be raised up at an angle to drain the fat.

The new, lightweight disk models have slotted surfaces fitted over shallow pans. The slots approximate grill marks on the food and allow the fat to run off. Liquid can be added to the pan to steam the food while it grills, which helps to keep it moist.

Asparagus Salad

*A*rranged on a single serving platter, this salad is a beautiful composition of vibrant color. It may be served as a first course or a side dish, and can add a festive touch to the buffet table.

Heating the blue cheese intensifies its flavor, making the most of a scant tablespoonful.

Serves 4

Fat per serving = 0.9 gram
Calories per serving = 71

28 asparagus spears (2 bundles), trimmed
½ cup plain nonfat yogurt
1 tablespoon crumbled blue cheese
¼ cup freshly squeezed lemon juice
1 tablespoon snipped fresh chives
1 garlic clove, peeled and minced
2 beefsteak tomatoes, cored and cut into wedges
Salt and freshly ground black pepper to taste
½ cup chopped fennel leaves (the feathery ends)

Bring water to a boil in the bottom of a steamer. Fit the basket into the steamer. Steam the asparagus over medium-high heat for about 6 minutes, until bright green and tender. Remove the steamer from the heat and let the asparagus cool.

Combine the yogurt and blue cheese in a small saucepan. Warm over low heat for 1 to 2 minutes, whisking constantly, just until the blue cheese has melted. Remove the pan from the heat and whisk in the lemon juice, chives, and garlic.

Arrange the asparagus in the center of a serving plate and ring with the tomato wedges. Drizzle the yogurt dressing over the asparagus. Sprinkle with salt and pepper and garnish with the fennel leaves.

Spinach Salad in Fresh Orange Dressing with Pine Nuts

*T*his unique and complex spinach salad teases the palate, juxtaposing the peppery watercress with a refreshing orange vinaigrette. The warm salad mixture is topped with cool orange segments, and toasted pine nuts provide a novel accent. I use white balsamic vinegar (which is sweeter and more delicate than regular balsamic), but you can substitute raspberry or any other of the wonderful fruit vinegars now on the market.

For added appeal, garnish each serving with an orange wheel.

Serves 4

Fat per serving = 3.1 grams
Calories per serving = 101

6 navel oranges, chilled
4 cups trimmed spinach (1 large bunch)
1½ cups trimmed watercress (1 bunch)
1 tablespoon pine nuts
⅓ cup minced shallot (2–3 large shallots)
2 garlic cloves, peeled and minced
5 tablespoons white balsamic vinegar
2 teaspoons sherry vinegar
Freshly ground black pepper to taste

Peel the oranges and remove the white pith. Over a bowl positioned to catch the juice, separate the segments of each orange from the membrane with a sharp knife, discarding the seeds, and set them aside. Squeeze the residual juice from the membranes into the bowl and reserve.

Combine the spinach and watercress in a mixing bowl.

Put the pine nuts in a small sauté pan and cook over medium heat for about 6 minutes, shaking the pan occasionally, until the nuts are golden brown. Transfer the pine nuts to a small bowl.

Put the shallots, garlic, vinegars, and reserved orange juice into the sauté pan. Bring to a boil over low heat. Stir in the black pepper, then pour the dressing over the spinach and watercress. Toss to coat.

Arrange the mixture on salad plates, spoon orange segments atop each, and garnish with the pine nuts and, if you like, orange wheels.

Making Orange Wheels

Slice an unpeeled orange into ¼-inch rounds. Make a cut halfway across each round, from the peel to the core, and twist the sides of the cut in opposite directions so that the top half of the round will stand upright when placed on the salad.

Selecting and Rinsing Spinach

In the market, choose spinach leaves that are small, firm, and dark green; if purchasing spinach by the bag, look for one marked "baby" or "salad" spinach.

To prepare, first discard any leaves that are wilted or discolored. Stem the spinach by folding each leaf lengthwise, then holding it in one hand, rib side out, and with the other hand pulling the stem off the leaf. Soak the spinach twice, "tickling" it each time—that is to say, gently massaging the leaves underwater to dislodge grit. Dry the spinach in a salad spinner or by wrapping the leaves in paper towels.

Preparing Romaine Lettuce

Select the crisp, medium green leaves from the head, discarding any dark green leaves, which have a slightly bitter taste. Rinse each leaf thoroughly under cold running water. For lettuce to be used in salads, rip the leaves into pieces and dry in a salad spinner. For sandwiches, pat dry each leaf individually.

Mock Caesar Salad

Gone here are the fat-laden oil and anchovies associated with traditional Caesar recipes, along with the increasingly suspect raw egg. In this version, tart Belgian endive lends a refreshingly pungent accent, while the tomatoes add an unexpected burst of color.

To crack black pepper, coarsely grind whole peppercorns in a mill or crush them lightly using a mortar and pestle.

2 garlic cloves, peeled and minced
¼ cup reduced-sodium soy sauce
¼ cup freshly squeezed lemon juice
3 cups chopped Belgian endive (4 heads)
6 cups torn Romaine lettuce (2 heads)
⅛ teaspoon freshly cracked black pepper
1 tablespoon freshly grated Parmesan cheese
1⅓ cups chopped tomato (1 large tomato)

Serves 4

Fat per serving =
1.2 grams
Calories per serving = 80

Put the garlic, soy sauce, and lemon juice in a salad bowl and whisk thoroughly. Add the endive and Romaine lettuce. Toss to coat. Sprinkle the black pepper and Parmesan cheese on top.

Garnish with the chopped tomato.

Curried Chicken Salad

I call for frozen peas in this recipe so that it can be made all year-round, but by all means use fresh if you're lucky enough to have your own garden. Lightly steam fresh peas, until they turn bright green, and then rinse them under cold running water.

This lively chicken salad is also good served in a pita pocket.

Serves 4

Fat per serving = 2.8 grams
Calories per serving = 200

1½ cups cubed cooked chicken breast (see Box, page 36)
¼ cup frozen peas, thawed
¼ cup scraped and shredded carrot
⅛ teaspoon celery seed
1 tablespoon golden raisins
1 cup shredded red cabbage
¼ cup chopped green apple
¼ cup chopped scallion (2–3 scallions)
¼ cup scraped and chopped celery

FOR THE DRESSING

1 cup plain nonfat yogurt
1 tablespoon nonfat mayonnaise
3 teaspoons curry powder
3 tablespoons freshly squeezed lemon juice

Freshly ground black pepper to taste
1 tablespoon Dijon-style mustard
2 tablespoons minced shallot (1 small shallot)

4 large red cabbage leaves
4 cherry tomatoes, halved
1 tablespoon chopped fresh parsley

Combine the chicken, peas, carrot, celery seed, raisins, shredded cabbage, apple, scallions, and celery in a salad bowl.

Put all the dressing ingredients in a small bowl and whisk to blend.

Pour the dressing over the salad and toss well. Cover and refrigerate for 1 hour.

Place a cabbage leaf, curved side down, on each salad plate. Mound salad into the leaves and garnish with the cherry tomatoes and parsley.

Poaching Chicken

2 cups dry white wine
2 cups water
2 sprigs fresh thyme or 1 tablespoon dried thyme
1 small onion, peeled and halved
1 boneless, skinless chicken breast

Put the wine, water, thyme, and onion in a deep-sided frying pan. Bring to a boil over medium heat and boil, uncovered, for 5 minutes. Add the chicken breast, cover, and simmer for 20 minutes.

All About Curries

Curry powders are spice mixtures that vary greatly in strength and taste, depending upon the mix of ingredients, which may include chile peppers, cumin, coriander, cardamom, black pepper, cloves, and turmeric. Some are mild; some, like madras curry powder, pack quite a wallop. I like to experiment when preparing curried chicken salad, varying the strength of the curry depending on whether the salad is to be a subtle side dish or an assertive main course.

Four Un-Fried Favorites

*B*eing raised a Southern girl—giving up fried foods hasn't been easy. Rosie has perfected un-frying my favorites, like chicken and catfish—meaning that the chicken is not fried but tastes like it is. You can use the same process for anything else you choose to un-fry.

We have served platters of skinless un-fried chicken to guests, and they thought it was the best fried chicken they ever had. You won't believe how good it is.

Oprah

Un-Fried Chicken

The secret to the success of this recipe is to make sure that both the chicken and the yogurt are very cold (hence, soaking the chicken in the ice water). The preliminary soaking will help the breading adhere and produce a crisp coating much like that of fried chicken.

If you're serving the chicken on a platter rather than on individual dinner plates, it looks smashing on a bed of flowering kale.

Light vegetable oil cooking spray
6 chicken drumsticks, skin removed
3 whole chicken breasts, halved and skin removed
3½ cups ice water
1 cup plain nonfat yogurt

FOR THE BREADING
1 cup dried Italian bread crumbs
1 cup all-purpose flour
1 tablespoon Old Bay seasoning
½ teaspoon garlic powder
½ teaspoon Creole seasoning
⅛ teaspoon freshly ground black pepper
Dash cayenne pepper

Makes 12 pieces

Fat per piece of breast = 2.2 grams
Calories per piece of breast = 185
Fat per drumstick = 4.2 grams
Calories per drumstick = 195

(continued on page 40)

(Un-Fried Chicken, continued)
½ teaspoon dried thyme
½ teaspoon dried basil
½ teaspoon dried oregano

Preheat the oven to 400 degrees.

Coat a baking sheet with 3 sprays of the vegetable oil.

Put the chicken in a large bowl with the ice water. Put the yogurt into a medium bowl. Set both bowls aside.

Toss all the breading ingredients into a large, tightly-sealing plastic bag. Seal and shake well to mix.

Remove 2 pieces of chicken from the ice water. Roll each piece in the yogurt. Put the chicken into the plastic bag, reseal, and shake to coat thoroughly. Transfer the breaded chicken to the prepared baking sheet. Repeat the process until all 12 pieces are breaded. Spray the chicken lightly with the vegetable oil.

Place the baking sheet on the bottom shelf of the oven and bake for 1 hour, turning the pieces every 20 minutes to allow even browning.

Serve hot or at room temperature.

Properly Handling
and Cooking Chicken

Raw chicken may contain bacteria that can cause illness. While the bacteria is destroyed by thorough cooking, care should be taken to avoid contaminating work surfaces and other foods with raw poultry juices and to ensure that the chicken is cooked properly.

Wash your hands, the cutting board, and any utensils that have come into contact with raw chicken in soap and hot water. Never return cooked chicken to a plate that may contain raw poultry juices, baste the bird with the liquid in which it has marinated, or use the marinade as a sauce unless the chicken has been cooked in the marinade.

Cook the chicken to 170 degrees on an instant-read thermometer, or until the juices run clear and you can no longer see any red or pink flesh once the meat pulls easily from the bone.

Un-Fried Catfish

I think this tastes just like fried catfish, but it has only a third of the calories and a sixth of the fat of the traditional version!

Garnish, if you wish, with sprigs of parsley tucked under the catfish fillets, or with lemon wedges. I like to cut the pointed ends off the lemon before cutting it into wedges, exposing more of the delicate fruit.

Serves 4

Fat per serving = 5.2 grams
Calories per serving = 172

Light vegetable oil cooking spray
¼ cup cornmeal
1 teaspoon dried thyme
1 teaspoon dried basil
½ teaspoon garlic powder
½ teaspoon lemon pepper
4 teaspoons blackening seasoning
Four 4-ounce catfish fillets
½ teaspoon paprika

Preheat the oven to 400 degrees.

Spray the vegetable oil over the baking sheet 3 times to coat.

Put the cornmeal, thyme, and basil on a large plate and mix well.

Sprinkle ⅛ teaspoon of the garlic powder, ⅛ teaspoon of the lemon pepper, and 1 teaspoon of the blackening seasoning on each of the catfish fillets. Coat the fillets thoroughly with the cornmeal mixture and transfer them to the prepared baking sheet. Dust each fillet with ⅛ teaspoon of the paprika. Coat the catfish lightly with the cooking spray.

Place the baking sheet on the bottom shelf of the oven. Bake for 20 minutes. Reduce the heat to 350 degrees and bake for about 5 minutes more, until the crust is golden and the fish flakes easily.

Un-Fried French Fries

*T*hese look almost as good as they taste. The Cajun spice lends a bright red hue to the crunchy surface, while the soft inside is snowy white. At half a gram of fat per serving (versus 16 grams for the same amount of the fried variety), you can munch away guiltlessly. Serve alongside a small bowl of reduced-calorie catsup.

Serves 4

Fat per serving = 0.5 gram
Calories per serving = 291

5 large baking potatoes (about 2¾ pounds total)
Light vegetable oil cooking spray
2 large egg whites
1 tablespoon Cajun spice

Preheat the oven to 400 degrees.

Slice each potato lengthwise into ¼-inch ovals, then slice each oval lengthwise into matchsticks.

Coat a baking sheet with 3 sprays of the vegetable oil.

Combine the egg whites and Cajun spice in a bowl. Add the matchstick potatoes and mix to coat. Pour the coated potatoes onto the prepared baking sheet and spread them out into a single layer, leaving a little space between.

Place the baking sheet on the bottom shelf of the oven. Bake for 40 to 45 minutes, until the fries are crispy, turning them every 6 to 8 minutes with a spatula so that they brown evenly. Serve immediately.

Un-Fried Crabcakes

Crabcakes are always a special treat. After eating mine, you'll never want the heavy fried kind again. With a little salad and some crackers, they make a satisfying meal.

1 pound fresh crabmeat (lump blue crab)
Light vegetable oil cooking spray
1 teaspoon freshly grated Parmesan cheese
1 tablespoon snipped fresh chives
1 large whole egg or 2 large egg whites, beaten
1 tablespoon Old Bay seasoning
1 teaspoon Italian seasoning
2 tablespoons chopped jalapeño pepper (1 large pepper)
1 teaspoon baking powder
2 tablespoons chopped fresh parsley
1 teaspoon Worcestershire sauce
1 cup unflavored dried bread crumbs

Serves 4

*Fat per serving =
  2.4 grams
Calories per serving = 252*

Preheat the oven to 400 degrees.

Rinse the crabmeat under cold running water and drain, making sure to remove any filament or shell.

Spray the vegetable oil over the baking sheet 3 times to coat.

In a large bowl, combine all remaining ingredients, except
(continued on page 46)

(Un-Fried Crabcakes, continued)

½ cup of the bread crumbs, and stir in the crabmeat. Using ¼ cup for each crabcake, form the mixture into 8 cakes. Roll each in the reserved bread crumbs and place on the prepared baking sheet. Coat the crabcakes lightly with the cooking spray.

Place the baking sheet on the bottom shelf of the oven and bake the crabcakes for about 5 minutes per side, until brown.

Pastas, Etc.

I *have thrived* on pasta. I can eat it every day and practically do. I ask Rosie to fix pasta at least 5 days a week. I never get tired of it.

There are so many different kinds—linguine, penne, rigatoni, fettucini, mostaccioli, papparadelle. Combine them with different sauces and the possibilities are virtually endless.

When I do take a break from pasta, one of Rosie's pizzas or a grilled vegetable sandwich on a crisp Italian roll can be a satisfying low-fat alternative.

Oprah

Penne with Sun-Dried Tomatoes and Chicken

*T*his filling pasta derives its distinctive character from smoky, intensely flavorful sun-dried tomatoes, a once rare treat now found in the produce section of most supermarkets. Buy the type packed dry in cellophane, rather than that packed in jars with oil.

If you grow your own basil, for added flecks of color, snip the crowns from the top of a few sprigs and scatter them over the pasta.

¼ cup sun-dried tomatoes
½ cup boiling water
6 ounces boneless, skinless chicken breast
¼ cup dry white wine
1 tablespoon Italian seasoning
3 tablespoons chopped shallot (1 large shallot)
1¼ cups chopped fresh portobello mushrooms (2 smallish mushrooms)
½ cup fresh peas or frozen peas, thawed
8 ounces dried penne
Light vegetable oil cooking spray
5 garlic cloves, peeled and minced
1 tablespoon all-purpose flour
12 ounces evaporated skim milk
⅛ teaspoon ground nutmeg

(continued on page 50)

Serves 4

*Fat per serving =
4.1 grams
Calories per serving =
435*

(Penne with Sun-Dried Tomatoes and Chicken, continued)
⅛ teaspoon crushed red pepper flakes
½ cup chopped fresh basil
5 medium black olives, thinly sliced

Preheat the oven to 350 degrees.

Put the sun-dried tomatoes in a bowl, add the boiling water, and set the bowl aside for the tomatoes to reconstitute.

Fill a large pot with water and bring it to a boil while proceeding with the recipe.

Combine the chicken and wine in a shallow baking dish. Sprinkle the Italian seasoning on top. Bake for 15 to 20 minutes, until the meat is no longer pink and the juices run clear. Remove and shred the chicken, reserving the cooking juices.

Drain the sun-dried tomatoes and slice them thinly.

Pour the reserved cooking juices from the chicken into a sauté pan. Add the shallots, mushrooms, peas, and the sliced sun-dried tomatoes. Sauté over low heat for a few minutes, until the liquid has been absorbed and the vegetables are wilted. Remove the pan from the heat and cover it to keep the vegetables warm.

Add the penne to the water in the large pot, which by now

A platter of Un-Fried Chicken with a Steamed Vegetable Platter accompaniment

*A bowl of Angel Hair Pasta with Lemon and Garlic, shown here with
extra shavings of Parmesan on top and a flower of yellow squash as a garnish*

should be at a full boil. Cook over high heat to desired doneness, 8 to 12 minutes.

While the pasta is cooking, make the sauce. Preheat a small, heavy saucepan for about 1 minute over medium heat, then spray it twice with the vegetable oil. Toss in the garlic and flour, then whisk in the evaporated milk. Add the nutmeg and red pepper flakes. Whisking constantly, bring the mixture to a boil and continue to cook for about 5 minutes, until thickened. Reduce the heat to the lowest setting and stir in the basil.

Drain the cooked pasta and transfer it to a warm serving bowl. Add the chicken, vegetables, and sauce. Toss and garnish with the sliced olives.

Substituting Chicken Stock for Oil

Tossing cooked pasta in a little chicken stock before adding the sauce lends the same silky texture to the pasta as would olive oil, with none of the fat. The stock lubricates the strands of pasta, keeping them from sticking together.

Pesto Linguine in Fresh Tomato Sauce

*R*ich and robust, this pasta has only a fraction of the fat and calories found in most pesto dishes. The bell pepper and carrot give the garlicky tomato sauce a pleasing hint of sweetness, while the jalapeño pepper lends a bit of fire.

For a spectacular presentation, top the pasta bowl with a few scallion starbursts.

Serves 4

Fat per serving = 3.8 grams
Calories per serving = 349

Light vegetable oil cooking spray
1 cup chopped onion (1 medium onion)
¼ cup chopped green bell pepper
¼ cup grated carrot
1 tablespoon dried oregano
1 tablespoon dried thyme
½ cup red wine
4½ cups peeled, seeded, and chopped plum tomatoes
  (about 2 pounds total)
2 tablespoons chopped jalapeño pepper (1 large pepper)
1 chicken bouillon cube
8 ounces dried linguine
7 garlic cloves, peeled and chopped
1 cup chopped mushrooms
1 tablespoon balsamic vinegar
1 tablespoon tomato paste
Salt and freshly ground black pepper to taste

2 tablespoons Rosie's pesto (see Box, page 57)
1 teaspoon freshly grated Parmesan cheese

Preheat a heavy sauté pan for about 1 minute over medium heat. Spray it 3 times with the vegetable oil. Toss in the onion, green pepper, and carrot and sauté for 2 minutes. Add the oregano, thyme, and wine. Cook for about 5 minutes, until most of the wine has been absorbed. Stir in the tomatoes, the jalapeño pepper, and the bouillon cube. Reduce the heat to low and simmer, uncovered, for 40 minutes, stirring occasionally.

In the meantime, bring a large pot of water to a boil over high heat. Once the water is boiling, add the linguine. Cook the pasta 8 to 12 minutes, to desired tenderness.

To the simmering vegetable mixture, add the garlic, mushrooms, vinegar, tomato paste, and salt and black pepper. Raise the heat to medium, cover, and cook for 10 minutes. Stir in the pesto.

When the linguine is done, drain and transfer it to a warm serving bowl. Add the sauce and toss. Garnish with the Parmesan cheese.

Making Scallion Starbursts

On each trimmed scallion, make 4 equidistant cuts from the top of the bulb about halfway down the scallion. Soak for 15 minutes in ice water, allowing the strands of scallion to curl open.

Spinach Fettucini with Ginger Chicken

*T*his is one of the prettiest pastas you'll ever see. Splashes of yellow squash and red bell pepper set off the green spinach noodles and the stark white bits of chicken. The dish has a distinctly Asian flavor, brimming with tantalizing fresh ginger.

Serves 4

Fat per serving = 3.9 grams
Calories per serving = 399

FOR THE MARINADE/DRESSING

⅓ cup chopped shallot (2 large shallots)
1 garlic clove, peeled and chopped
⅛ teaspoon crushed red pepper flakes
1 teaspoon dried thyme
2 teaspoons freshly squeezed lime juice
1 tablespoon Dijon-style mustard
2 tablespoons reduced-sodium soy sauce
2 tablespoons rice wine vinegar
¼ cup dry white wine
2 teaspoons honey
3 tablespoons grated fresh ginger

8 ounces boneless, skinless chicken breast
8 ounces dried spinach fettucini
½ cup chicken stock, fat skimmed off
1 medium yellow squash, trimmed and
    cut into matchsticks

1 medium red bell pepper, trimmed and cut into strips
1 large leek, white part only, trimmed and cut
into 1-inch half rounds
2 cups broccoli florets (1 bundle)
1 cup chopped mushrooms
¼ cup snipped fresh chives

Preheat the oven to 350 degrees.

Put all the marinade/dressing ingredients in a blender and mix thoroughly at low speed.

Place the chicken in a shallow baking dish. Pour half of the mixture from the blender over the poultry, reserving the remainder. Cover and refrigerate the chicken for 20 minutes.

While the chicken is marinating, bring a large pot of water to a boil over high heat. Add the fettucini and cook for 8 to 12 minutes, to desired doneness.

In the meantime, remove the chicken from the refrigerator. Uncover the baking dish and transfer it to the oven. Bake for about 15 minutes, until the meat is no longer pink and the juices run clear.

When the pasta is cooked, remove the pot from the heat. Drain the fettucini and return it to the pot. Stir in the chicken stock and keep the mixture warm over the lowest heat setting.

(continued on page 56)

(Spinach Fettucini with Ginger Chicken, continued)

Pour the cooking juices from the chicken into a sauté pan. Add the squash, bell pepper, leek, broccoli, and mushrooms. Sauté for about 3 minutes, just until the vegetables begin to wilt.

Transfer the pasta to a warm serving bowl, along with the vegetables. Shred the chicken on top. Add the reserved dressing and toss. Garnish with the snipped chives.

Fresh vs. Dried Pasta

I prefer dried pasta to fresh for several reasons, not the least of which is that it lacks the fat and cholesterol of the fresh variety, which is made with eggs. Better-quality dried pastas can be purchased in a seemingly endless range of flavors—usually at a fraction of the price of fresh. They hold up to the most robust of sauces and are simpler to cook.

If you use fresh pasta, be sure to separate the strands before adding them to the pot so that they don't stick together while cooking. Time carefully. Fresh pasta is done in 3 to 5 minutes and can be overcooked easily.

Rosie's Pesto

I make pesto in volume during the summer, when fresh basil is bountiful, and freeze it in ¼-cup quantities for use year-round. You need only just enough pesto to coat the pasta lightly, as a little of this intensely flavorful mixture goes a long way.

1½ cups fresh basil leaves
2–5 garlic cloves, peeled *
¼ cup pine nuts
¼ cup freshly grated Parmesan cheese
¼ cup freshly squeezed lemon juice

Put the basil, garlic, pine nuts, and Parmesan cheese in a blender or food processor. Turn the machine on and drizzle in the lemon juice. Continue to puree until a smooth paste is formed.

Makes ¾ cup pesto

Fat per ½ tablespoon = 1.1 grams
Calories per ½ tablespoon = 14

* The amount of garlic you use is a matter of personal taste. Also, some garlic is more pungent. So start perhaps with 2 medium cloves, then taste, and add more if, as I do, you like a strong, garlicky flavor.

Angel Hair Pasta
with Lemon and Garlic

*D*elicate angel hair pasta demands a light and elegant sauce, such as this simple white wine mixture flecked with bits of fresh tomato and basil. It's a terrific first course or luncheon dish. I find the spinach and semolina varieties to be somewhat sturdier than plain wheat-flour angel hair pasta, but you still need to handle them carefully. Cook for only 30 seconds to 1 minute, toss, and serve immediately.

Serves 4

Fat per serving =
4.1 grams
Calories per serving = 291

1 teaspoon olive oil
2 garlic cloves, peeled and minced
½ cup dry white wine
¼ cup freshly squeezed lemon juice
1 cup chopped tomato (1 medium tomato)
4 ounces dried spinach angel hair pasta
4 ounces dried semolina angel hair pasta
¼ cup chopped fresh basil
2 tablespoons freshly grated Parmesan cheese
Freshly ground black pepper to taste

Bring a large pot of water to a boil over high heat and maintain at a boil.

Put the olive oil and garlic in a sauté pan and cook over medium heat just until the garlic begins to brown. Remove the sauté pan from the heat and pour in the wine. Return it to the heat. Cook for another 1 to 2 minutes, until the wine has been reduced by half. Stir in the lemon juice and tomato. Remove the pan from the heat.

Place the pasta in the boiling water and cook to desired doneness, 30 seconds to 1 minute. Drain the pasta and put it into a warm serving bowl. Add the basil, Parmesan cheese, and black pepper, along with the tomato mixture. Toss and serve immediately.

Bow Tie Pasta
with Blackened Scallops

*A*n extravaganza for the eye and the palate, this dish teams spicy blackened scallops with whimsical bow tie pasta in a novel cilantro-walnut pesto. It's topped by a roasted red pepper sauce that's as vibrant as it is pungent.

The seafood stock can be made from fish-flavored bouillon cubes available in most supermarkets.

Serves 4

Fat per serving =
4.0 grams
Calories per serving = 314

FOR THE PEPPER SAUCE

2 roasted red bell peppers (see Box, page 77)
⅓ cup chopped shallot (2 large shallots)
1 garlic clove, peeled and chopped
1 tablespoon sherry vinegar
½ cup seafood stock
2 tablespoons chopped fresh basil or 1 tablespoon dried basil

FOR THE CILANTRO PESTO

2 tablespoons chopped walnuts
2–3 garlic cloves, peeled
1½ cups fresh cilantro leaves (2 bunches)
¼ cup seafood stock
3 tablespoons freshly squeezed lemon juice

8 ounces dried bow tie (butterfly) pasta
16 large sea scallops (about 1 pound)
4 tablespoons blackening seasoning
1 tablespoon paprika
1 teaspoon dried thyme
½ lemon

Bring a large pot of water to a boil over high heat.

In the meantime, make the sauce. Put the roasted peppers, shallots, garlic, and vinegar in a blender and puree until smooth. Add ½ cup seafood stock and the basil and mix until blended. Transfer the mixture to a small saucepan, cover, and warm over the lowest heat setting.

For the cilantro pesto, put the walnuts, garlic, and cilantro in the bowl of a food processor. Turn the machine on and add 1 tablespoon of the seafood stock through the feed tube. Drizzle in the lemon juice to form a paste. Transfer the contents of the food processor to a small mixing bowl and whisk in another 3 tablespoons of the stock.

When the water comes to a boil, add the pasta to the pot. Cook for 8 to 10 minutes, to desired tenderness. Drain.

(continued on page 62)

(Bow Tie Pasta with Blackened Scallops, continued)

Dust the scallops with the blackening seasoning, paprika, and thyme. Heat a heavy frying pan for 2 to 3 minutes over medium heat. Spray the pan with vegetable oil. Add the prepared scallops and sear them for 2 minutes on each side. Reduce the heat to low and squeeze the lemon over the scallops. Cover and cook for about 5 minutes, until the scallops are firm.

Return the drained pasta to the pot. Over low heat, stir in the cilantro pesto.

Divide the pasta among 4 bowls. Place 4 scallops on top of each and pour the pepper sauce over the scallops.

Pasta in White Clam Sauce

A low-fat buttermilk-and-cornstarch mixture is the
key to this pasta's creamy white sauce. Sweet canned
clams provide a pleasing contrast to the tartness of the buttermilk. The fresh clams served in their shells lend visual
excitement to the dish; for added effect, surround them with
slices of red bell pepper.

8 ounces dried spaghetti
½ cup dry white wine
¼ cup water
⅓ cup chopped shallot (2 large shallots)
3 garlic cloves, peeled and minced
12 littleneck clams
10 ounces canned baby clams, broth reserved
1 cup low-fat buttermilk
1 teaspoon cornstarch dissolved in 2 teaspoons water
4 teaspoons freshly grated Parmesan cheese
1 teaspoon dried oregano
3 tablespoons chopped fresh basil
⅛ teaspoon ground white pepper
1 teaspoon Louisiana-style hot sauce
2 tablespoons chopped fresh parsley

Serves 4

*Fat per serving =
3.6 grams
Calories per serving =
375*

(continued on page 64)

(Pasta in White Clam Sauce, continued)

Bring a large pot of water to a boil over high heat, add the spaghetti, and cook to desired doneness, 6 to 9 minutes. Drain.

Meanwhile, put the wine, water, shallots, and garlic in a medium saucepan and bring to a boil over medium heat. Add the fresh clams, cover, and continue to cook over medium heat. Remove the clams when their shells have opened. Stir the broth from the canned clams into the saucepan. Cook a few minutes more, until the liquid is reduced by half.

Reduce the heat to low and whisk in the buttermilk-and-cornstarch mixture. Cook for about 2 minutes more to thicken, whisking constantly. Stir in the Parmesan cheese, canned clams, oregano, basil, pepper, hot sauce, and chopped parsley.

Combine the pasta and the clam sauce in a warm serving bowl and toss to coat. Garnish with the cooked clams, in their shells.

Individual Pizzas
with Three Topping Variations

No longer limited to the realm of sausage and mounds of fatty cheese, today's light pizzas please the palate with an array of sophisticated flavor combinations. Consider the three variations that follow as departure points, knowing that you can mix and match ingredients guiltlessly according to whim. Oprah likes the works!

Pizza Dough

¾ cup lukewarm water
1 teaspoon honey
1 tablespoon dry active yeast
1½ cups all-purpose flour
½ cup semolina
½ teaspoon salt
1 teaspoon olive oil
½ cup cornmeal
Light vegetable oil cooking spray

Makes 8 individual pizza crusts

Mix the water and honey together in a medium stainless steel bowl. Sprinkle the yeast on top and set it aside for about 20 minutes to proof, until bubbles form on the surface.

(continued on page 66)

(Pizza Dough, continued)

Put the flour, semolina, and salt into the bowl of a food processor. Turn the machine on and slowly add the yeast mixture through the feed tube. Process for about a minute, until a dough ball forms, drizzling a little additional water into the feed tube if necessary. Continue to process for another 2 minutes.

Rub the surface of a large bowl with the olive oil. Transfer the dough ball to the bowl and roll it in the oil to coat. Cover with a towel and set the bowl aside in a warm place until the dough has doubled in size, about 1 hour.

Preheat the oven to 400 degrees.

Remove the dough to a work surface that has been dusted with the cornmeal and roll out evenly to a thickness of about ¼ inch. Cut out eight 5½-inch circles, using a sharp knife and a saucer of that circumference.

Spray a cookie sheet 3 times with the vegetable oil to coat and put the pizza rounds onto the sheet. Bake for 3 to 5 minutes, until golden. Remove the baked crusts from the oven and add the topping variation of your choice.

Rosie finishing the tomato sauce and pouring it onto angel hair pasta

Rosie putting a tray of eggplant slices into the oven to roast

Individual Pesto Pizzas
with Mushrooms and Olives

¼ cup Rosie's pesto (see Box, page 57)
8 baked individual pizza crusts (see pages 65–6)
8 large spinach leaves, trimmed
½ cup Rosie's pizza sauce (see Box, page 69)
½ cup shredded nonfat mozzarella cheese
6 small mushrooms, thinly sliced
5 black olives, thinly sliced
1 tablespoon freshly grated Parmesan cheese

*Makes eight
5½-inch pizzas*

*Fat per pizza = 3.3 grams
Calories per pizza = 232*

Preheat the oven to 400 degrees.

Spread ½ tablespoon of the pesto on each of the pizza crusts. Lay a spinach leaf on top and cover with 1 tablespoon of the pizza sauce. Over the sauce, scatter 1 tablespoon of mozzarella cheese, then equal amounts of the sliced mushrooms and olives. Finish with a light sprinkling of the Parmesan cheese.

Place the pizzas on a cookie sheet and bake for 10 minutes.

Individual Goat Cheese Pizzas with Artichokes and Onion

*Makes eight
5½-inch pizzas*

*Fat per pizza = 3.5 grams
Calories per pizza = 190*

8 baked individual pizza crusts (see pages 65–6)
¼ cup crumbled chèvre (goat cheese)
16 whole fresh basil leaves
7 canned artichoke hearts, drained and sliced
1 small onion, trimmed and cut into thin rounds
1 large tomato, cored and cut into 8 slices
¼ cup Italian seasoning

Preheat the oven to 400 degrees.

Spread ½ tablespoon chèvre on each pizza crust. Layer 2 basil leaves, 1 tablespoon artichoke hearts, ½ tablespoon onion, a slice of tomato, and ½ tablespoon Italian seasoning.

Place the pizzas on a cookie sheet and bake for 10 minutes.

Rosie's Pizza Sauce

This spicy concoction packs a kick, courtesy of its generous mixture of dried herbs and red pepper flakes. A far cry from your typically bland pizza sauce, it's virtually fat free and can be made in minutes.

1 tablespoon tomato paste
1 cup tomato puree
⅛ teaspoon crushed red pepper flakes
2 teaspoons dried oregano
2 teaspoons dried basil
2 teaspoons dried thyme

Combine all the ingredients in a small saucepan and cook over low heat for about 15 minutes, until the sauce thickens.

Makes ½ cup sauce

Fat per tablespoon = 0.1 gram
Calories per tablespoon = 18

Individual Mixed Vegetable Pizzas with Blue Cheese

Makes eight 5½-inch pizzas

*Fat per pizza = 4.3 grams
Calories per pizza = 229*

½ cup sun-dried tomatoes
1 cup boiling water
1 small eggplant, trimmed and peeled
1 large zucchini, trimmed
Cayenne pepper to taste
Light vegetable oil cooking spray
1 roasted red bell pepper and 1 roasted yellow
    bell pepper (see Box, page 77)
8 baked individual pizza crusts (see pages 65–6)
¼ cup Rosie's pesto (see Box, page 57)
½ cup Rosie's pizza sauce (see Box, page 69)
¼ cup crumbled blue cheese

Preheat the broiler.

Put the sun-dried tomatoes in a small bowl and reconstitute by adding the boiling water and letting them soak for a few minutes.

Slice both the eggplant and the zucchini into ¼-inch rounds. Sprinkle with cayenne if desired. Place the rounds on the broiler rack and lightly coat with the cooking spray. Broil for 3 to 5 minutes, until brown. Flip the slices, spray the second side, and broil until brown. Remove the vegetables from the broiler. Set the oven to 400 degrees.

Slice the roasted peppers into thin strips. Drain the sun-dried tomatoes.

On each of the pizza crusts, spread ½ tablespoon pesto and 1 tablespoon pizza sauce. Scatter a few slices of eggplant, zucchini, roasted peppers, and sun-dried tomatoes over the pesto. Top each pizza with ½ tablespoon of the blue cheese.

Place the pizzas on a cookie sheet and bake for about 10 minutes, until the cheese is bubbly.

Bruschetta with Chopped Tomato Salad

Crusty toasted bread infused with garlic and sometimes topped with any of a variety of seasonings and seasonal ingredients, bruschetta is a classic Italian treat. I've made two changes in the traditional Tuscan version on which this recipe is based: I've omitted the typically generous addition of fatty oil and I've used as toppings a zesty salad mixture that can be spooned onto the bruschetta as desired.

Serves 4

Fat per serving =
2.2 grams
Calories per serving = 209

FOR THE SALAD

2 cups chopped tomato (2 medium tomatoes)
1 cup chopped red bell pepper (1 medium pepper)
1 cup chopped yellow bell pepper (1 medium pepper)
1 cup chopped onion (1 medium onion)
2 teaspoons capers
3 tablespoons chopped fresh basil
1 tablespoon balsamic vinegar
2 teaspoons freshly squeezed lemon juice
Freshly ground black pepper to taste
1 garlic clove, peeled and minced
1 teaspoon dried oregano

8 slices pizza dough baguette (see Box, page 74)
3 garlic cloves, peeled and halved lengthwise

Put all the salad ingredients in a large mixing bowl and toss thoroughly. Cover and refrigerate for 1 hour.

Preheat the broiler.

Arrange the bread on the broiler rack and broil about 2 minutes per side, until browned. Remove the bread slices and rub them with the cut side of the garlic halves. Discard the garlic.

Place a mound of salad on each serving plate, with 2 slices of bruschetta alongside.

Pizza Dough Baguettes

I use pizza dough to make great, hearty baguettes for my bruschetta and grilled vegetable sandwiches. To yield two 9-inch baguettes, follow the recipe for pizza dough (pages 65–6) up to the point at which the dough has risen for an hour, to double its original size.

Transfer the dough to a work surface that has been dusted with cornmeal. Knead the dough for about 5 minutes, until elastic, repeatedly pushing it away from you with the palm of your hand, then folding it over toward you, and pushing it away again in a wavelike motion.

Cut the dough in half. With the palms of your hands, roll each piece into a narrow rope 9 inches long. Spray a cookie sheet 3 times with light vegetable oil cooking spray and place the dough on the sheet. Cover with a towel and put the cookie sheet in a warm spot until the halves of dough double in size, 30 to 40 minutes.

Toward the end of this second rise, preheat the oven to 375 degrees.

With a razor blade, make 3 diagonal slashes on the top of each baguette. Sprinkle 1 teaspoon of all-purpose flour over each. Bake for about 25 minutes, until the baguettes are brown and sound hollow when tapped.

Transfer the baguettes to a wire rack to cool.

Grilled Vegetable Sandwich

*T*his tongue-tingling creation features a colorful and rather monumental assemblage of warm vegetables atop layers of fresh tomato, basil leaves, arugula, and roasted peppers—smothered in a spicy mustard-yogurt dressing and spiked with liberal applications of cayenne and black pepper, jalapeño peppers, and Tabasco sauce. So much for preconceptions of healthy food as bland and unsatisfying.

I usually grill the vegetables but have adapted recipe directions for the broiler to make it easier to do in the kitchen.

FOR THE DRESSING

1 cup plain nonfat yogurt
3 tablespoons Dijon-style mustard
Freshly ground black pepper to taste
2 tablespoons nonfat cottage cheese
⅛ teaspoon Tabasco sauce
2 tablespoons minced shallot (1 small shallot)
1 garlic clove, peeled and minced
1 teaspoon freshly squeezed lemon juice

1 small eggplant, trimmed and cut into ¼-inch rounds
1 medium yellow squash, trimmed and cut into ¼-inch rounds

Serves 6

Fat per serving = 3.2 grams
Calories per serving = 258

(continued on page 76)

(Grilled Vegetable Sandwich, continued)

1 medium zucchini, trimmed and cut into
  ¼-inch rounds
1 red onion, trimmed and cut into ¼-inch rounds
3 teaspoons Italian seasoning
⅛ teaspoon cayenne pepper
Light vegetable oil cooking spray
2 roasted red bell peppers (see Box, opposite)
2 pizza dough baguettes (see Box, page 74)
1 large tomato, cored and sliced
Freshly ground black pepper to taste
2 tablespoons chopped jalapeño pepper (1 large pepper)
8 fresh basil leaves
8 arugula leaves

Preheat the broiler.

Put all the dressing ingredients in a blender and mix at low speed until smooth. Set aside.

Arrange the eggplant, yellow squash, zucchini, and onion in a single layer on a cookie sheet. Sprinkle the Italian seasoning and cayenne pepper over all of the rounds. Spray the vegetable oil over to coat lightly. Broil the vegetables for about 5 minutes, until brown, turn the rounds over, and brown the other side. Remove the cookie sheet, leaving the broiler on.

Quarter the roasted bell peppers.

Cut each of the baguettes in half lengthwise and scoop out the soft inner dough. Place them on the broiler rack and toast for about 2 minutes per side.

Put a few slices of tomato into the well in the bottom of each baguette. Dust with black pepper and jalapeño pepper. Place 4 basil leaves, 4 arugula leaves, and 4 pieces of roasted pepper on each baguette. Layer on slices of eggplant, yellow squash, zucchini, and onion. Coat the inside of the remaining half of each baguette with the dressing and place it on top of the vegetables. Cut each baguette into 3 sandwiches.

Roasting Bell Peppers

Roasting brings out the natural sweetness of bell peppers and imparts a slightly smoky taste. And it's really a quick and easy procedure.

Slice the peppers in half lengthwise, core, and remove the seeds. Put the sliced peppers on the rack of a preheated broiler, cut side down. Broil for about 5 minutes, until the skin blisters.

Transfer the roasted peppers to a tightly-sealing plastic bag, close it, and leave them for 10 or 15 minutes. When cool, the charred skin can be rubbed easily from the peppers and discarded.

Entrees

I **love it when** friends come over for dinner. They have to eat like I eat. I have been able to introduce them to a healthier way of eating without them even knowing it. They don't seem to miss the fat, and they always ask for seconds. One that always renders a round of applause and also makes a handsome centerpiece for the simplest or most sophisticated is Rosie's paella dinner. And the bonus is that it tastes as rich and satisfying as it looks.

Oprah

Paella

*I*n this beautiful dish jet-black mussels, pale gray clams, and vibrant red lobster tails lie on a bed of golden saffron rice, surrounded by chopped tomato and green peas, its flavor enhanced by the addition of squid rings and an assortment of peppers.

½ cup dry white wine
3 tablespoons saffron threads*
Light vegetable oil cooking spray
1 cup chopped onion (1 medium onion)
1 cup arborio rice
1 banana pepper, trimmed and cut into strips
1 red bell pepper, trimmed and cut into strips
1 yellow bell pepper, trimmed and cut into strips
3 cups hot chicken stock, fat skimmed off
6 ounces boneless, skinless chicken breast, cubed
½ cup squid rings
½ pound medium shrimp, peeled and deveined
12 mussels, scrubbed
12 littleneck clams, scrubbed
Four 3-ounce freshwater lobster tails, or two 6-ounce lobster tails cut in half
½ cup canned sliced artichoke hearts
1 cup frozen peas, thawed
1 cup chopped tomato (1 medium tomato)

(continued on page 82)

Serves 4

Fat per serving = 4.3 grams
Calories per serving = 477

(Paella, continued)

Preheat the oven to 350 degrees.

Put the white wine and saffron threads in a small bowl and set aside.

Preheat a large, heavy paella pan or frying pan for about 1 minute over medium-high heat. Spray it 4 times with the vegetable oil. Sauté the onion for 2 to 3 minutes, until limp. Add the rice and sauté for about 1 minute, until golden. Add the wine and saffron and stir until the liquid is completely absorbed. Stir in the peppers. Add the hot chicken stock ¼ cup at a time, stirring until absorbed. Keep the stock over low heat. When only ½ cup of the chicken stock remains to be added, stir in the chicken. With the last addition of stock, stir in the squid and shrimp. Turn the burner off. The rice should be tender.

Stand the mussels and clams upright in the rice mixture, joint down. Tuck the lobster tails into the rice, shell down. Transfer the pan to the oven and bake until the mussel and clam shells open, 8 to 10 minutes.

Scatter the artichoke, peas, and tomato over the paella and bake for 2 to 3 minutes more.

Place the paella in the center of the dinner table and allow the guests to serve themselves.

*Saffron threads are loosely measured, not packed down so 3 tablespoons is not too much. However, if they're too expensive, use less or leave them out entirely.

Roast Chicken
with Seed Bread Stuffing

Classic fare for a Sunday afternoon gathering of family and friends, this updated rendition is considerably healthier than the traditional menu on which it is based. The stuffing is roasted on the side so as not to absorb fat from the cavity of the bird, the chicken is skinned before serving, and no oil or butter is used in preparing either.

To serve, twist about ⅔ of the inner leaves out of a head of purple flowering kale. Place the hollow shell in the center of a platter and fill it with the stuffing. Ring with the severed leaves to form a bed for the chicken. Garnish the platter with chopped yellow bell pepper.

3 large carrots, trimmed, peeled, and cut into large chunks
3 stalks celery, trimmed, scraped, and cut into large chunks
1 large onion, trimmed, peeled, and cut into large chunks
One 4-pound roasting chicken, split in half
5 large garlic cloves, peeled and halved lengthwise
1 medium lemon
1 tablespoon chopped fresh tarragon
½ teaspoon paprika
½ teaspoon seasoned salt
½ teaspoon freshly ground black pepper
½ teaspoon lemon pepper

Serves 8

*Fat per serving =
5.7 grams
Calories per serving = 317*

(continued on page 84)

(Roast Chicken with Seed Bread Stuffing, continued)

FOR THE STUFFING

½ cup chicken stock, fat skimmed off
Light vegetable oil cooking spray
1 cup chopped onion (1 medium onion)
2 garlic cloves, peeled and minced
1 cup minced mushrooms
1 cup scraped and chopped celery (2 medium stalks)
1 cup dry white wine
6 cups toasted light-wheat-bread cubes
1 cup chopped green apple (1 apple)
¼ cup seedless raisins
2 teaspoons poppy seeds
2 teaspoons sunflower seeds
⅛ teaspoon ground sage
⅛ teaspoon freshly ground black pepper
Cayenne pepper to taste
2 large egg whites, beaten

Preheat the oven to 350 degrees.

Scatter the carrots, celery, and onion in a roasting pan. Place the halves of chicken, skin side up, on the vegetables. Randomly tuck 5 pieces of garlic under the skin on each half. Squeeze the lemon over the chicken. Dust with the tarragon, paprika, seasoned salt, and peppers. Cover and put in the oven.

Make the stuffing while the chicken is cooking. Put the chicken stock in a small saucepan over the lowest heat.

Preheat a medium, heavy frying pan for about 1 minute over medium heat. Spray it twice with the vegetable oil. Add the onion, garlic, mushrooms, and celery. Sauté for 3 minutes. Add the wine and cook for 2 to 3 minutes more, until the vegetables are limp. Remove the pan from the heat.

Combine the bread, apple, raisins, poppy seeds, sunflower seeds, sage, and peppers in a large bowl and toss to mix. Add the warm chicken stock, the vegetable mixture, and the egg whites. Mix thoroughly with a wooden spoon. Pour the stuffing mixture into a casserole and cover.

When the chicken has cooked for 15 minutes, put the casserole of stuffing in the oven and bake alongside the chicken.

When the chicken has cooked 45 minutes, uncover, baste lightly with pan juices, and return the roasting pan to the oven uncovered. Now bake both for 15 minutes, or until the thigh juices of the chicken run clear. Total cooking time for the chicken is 1 hour; 45 minutes for the stuffing.

Remove the skin and carve the meat from the bones.

Peppered Tuna Niçoise

Here pepper-coated lean yellowfin tuna is seared until crusty, creating a striking visual accent to the deep red flesh of the fish. In lieu of the oil-based dressing commonly used on salade Niçoise, I've created an Asian-inspired orange-and-ginger mixture that gets an added boost from wasabi, the powerful Japanese horseradish powder.

Serves 4

*Fat per serving =
2.8 grams
Calories per serving = 310*

FOR THE DRESSING

¼ cup rice wine vinegar
¼ teaspoon wasabi powder
1 teaspoon fresh thyme leaves
1 small shallot, trimmed and quartered
2 tablespoons chopped fresh ginger
2 teaspoons chopped fresh basil leaves
½ cup freshly squeezed orange juice

6 cups mixed salad greens
½ cup sliced radishes
8 small new white potatoes, thinly sliced
1 cup trimmed string beans
4 tablespoons coarsely ground black pepper
Four 6-ounce yellowfin (ahi) tuna fillets (about
    ½-inch thick)
4 Spanish green olives, pitted and sliced
¼ red bell pepper, trimmed and cut into thin strips
4 lemon wedges

Put all the dressing ingredients except the orange juice in a blender or food processor. Turn the machine on. Once the shallot is finely chopped, drizzle in the juice.

Toss the salad greens and radishes together until well mixed and divide among 4 salad plates.

Bring water to a boil in the bottom of a steamer. Put the potatoes and beans in the steamer basket, and steam until fork tender, about 15 minutes. Remove from the heat and allow the vegetables to cool.

Sprinkle ½ tablespoon of the black pepper on each of the tuna fillets and press it into the fish. Turn the tuna and press another ½ tablespoon pepper into the flip side of each.

Preheat a large, heavy (preferably cast-iron) frying pan over medium heat for 2 to 3 minutes, until very hot. Put the tuna into the pan in a single layer, and cook for 2 minutes per side, just until blackened and firm to the touch (but still pink inside when cut into).

Slice the tuna and arrange it atop the greens, along with the potatoes and string beans. Garnish with the sliced olives and red pepper strips. Drizzle the dressing over all and add a lemon wedge to each plate.

Skewered Shrimp
on Wild Rice Pilaf

A little coconut milk is used to temper the hot mix of chile paste, coriander, and garlic in the shrimp marinade, lending a hint of sweetness to this dish. The spicy shrimp are served on a bed of soothing rice pilaf. I've added a bit of crunch to the fluffy rice mixture in the form of toasted millet, a high-protein grain.

Serves 4

Fat per serving = 4.8 grams
Calories per serving = 324

FOR THE RICE PILAF

¼ cup millet
Light vegetable oil cooking spray
½ cup chopped onion (1 small onion)
¼ cup scraped and chopped carrot (1 small carrot)
¼ cup scraped and chopped celery
¼ cup chopped red bell pepper
¼ cup wild rice
½ cup brown rice
2¼ cups chicken stock, fat skimmed off
1 tablespoon reduced-sodium soy sauce

2 tablespoons coconut milk
1 teaspoon chile paste (no-oil variety)
2 garlic cloves, peeled and minced
1 teaspoon dried coriander
1 teaspoon lime zest

16 medium shrimp (about 8 ounces),
peeled and deveined
1 large onion, trimmed and cut into 16 chunks
16 cherry tomatoes
16 small mushrooms, trimmed
1 large red bell pepper, trimmed and cut
into twelve 2-inch cubes
1 large yellow bell pepper, trimmed and cut
into twelve 2-inch cubes

Put the millet into a medium frying pan and cook for about 2 minutes over medium heat, stirring constantly, until toasted.

Preheat a medium, heavy stainless steel saucepan for about 1 minute over medium heat. Spray it 3 times with the vegetable oil. Add the onion, carrot, celery, and the chopped bell pepper. Sauté for about 3 minutes, until the vegetables are limp. Add the toasted millet, the wild rice, and the brown rice. Add the chicken stock and soy sauce, stir once, and bring to a boil over high heat. Cover, reduce the heat to low, and simmer for 45 minutes.

While the rice is cooking, combine the coconut milk, chile paste, garlic, coriander, and lime zest in a mixing

(continued on page 90)

(Skewered Shrimp on Wild Rice Pilaf, continued)

bowl. Whisk thoroughly. Add the shrimp, onion, tomatoes, mushrooms, and peppers, and toss to coat. Cover and marinate the shrimp in the refrigerator for 30 minutes.

Preheat a grill or broiler.

On each of 8 small skewers, thread 2 pieces of drained shrimp, 2 chunks of onion, 2 cherry tomatoes, 2 mushrooms, and 3 bell pepper cubes. Alternate ingredients on the skewers, placing a bell pepper cube at each end. Grill or broil the skewers for 4 minutes, turn, and cook for another 4 to 6 minutes, until the shrimp are bright pink and the vegetables are slightly charred.

Fluff the rice pilaf and divide it among 4 warm dinner plates. Place the skewers on top.

Choosing a Duck

It's worth the trip to a meat market or specialty grocer for Muscovy duck breast, since most supermarkets stock only whole ducks of the fatty Long Island variety. Muscovy duck, which is as lean as Muschicken, is sold as boneless breast meat. It's easier and considerably less messy to cook, and you won't have to bother with cumbersome carving. Don't be intimidated by the price per pound; remember that you are paying only for a firm, boneless breast that will serve four easily.

Roasted Duck Breast with Pineapple Chutney

*E*legant dinner party fare made easy, this spectacular dish can be prepared in a little over an hour. I've never understood why more people don't cook duck at home; but because they don't, it's always welcomed as a special treat.

I serve the duck medium rare. If you prefer well done, roast the duck for 10 minutes in a preheated 350-degree oven after completing recipe directions for grilling or broiling.

Serves 4

*Fat per serving =
4.6 grams*
Calories per serving = 248

FOR THE MARINADE

2 teaspoons chile paste (no-oil variety)
3 tablespoons reduced-sodium soy sauce
3 tablespoons freshly squeezed lime juice
1 tablespoon honey
¼ cup unsweetened pineapple juice

One 14-ounce skinless Muscovy duck breast

FOR THE CHUTNEY

1½ cups small cubes fresh pineapple
½ teaspoon lime zest
Pulp of 1 large lime
¾ cup unsweetened pineapple juice
½ tablespoon chopped crystallized ginger
½ tablespoon chopped jalapeño pepper

2 tablespoons golden raisins
¼ cup chopped red bell pepper
½ cup chopped red onion
2 tablespoons white wine vinegar

Mix all the marinade ingredients in a large bowl. Put the duck breast into the marinade, cover, and refrigerate for at least 1 hour.

In the meantime, bring all the chutney ingredients to a boil in a medium saucepan over medium heat. Reduce the heat to low and simmer, uncovered, until the fruit is tender and the sauce has thickened, about 45 minutes. Stir occasionally.

Preheat a grill or broiler when the chutney is almost done.

Grill or broil the duck for about 5 minutes on each side, until a light crust forms and the meat inside is pink. Slice into 16 medallions.

Fan 4 medallions on each serving plate and spoon chutney over.

Red Beans and Rice with Salsa

*A*n abundance of dried herbs and spices, garlic, and onion tantalize the tongue with every mouthful of this potent pairing of nutritious, high-protein beans and rice. I serve it with fish or poultry, or as a wintertime one-dish meal. For even more zest, garnish each serving with a generous sprinkle of chopped fresh cilantro.

Serves 6

Fat per serving = 2.1 grams
Calories per serving = 278

½ cup dried red beans
½ cup dried kidney beans
3 cups water
1½ cups chopped onion (1–2 onions)
3 garlic cloves, peeled and halved lengthwise
1 teaspoon dried oregano
1 bay leaf
2 tablespoons chili powder
1 teaspoon ground cumin
1 teaspoon dried coriander
1 teaspoon crushed red pepper flakes
1 cup tomato juice
1 cup brown rice
2 cups chicken stock, fat skimmed off

FOR THE SALSA

1½ cups cubed tomato (1 large tomato)
2 tablespoons minced jalapeño pepper (1 large pepper)
¼ cup sliced scallion, white part only (2 large scallions)

¼ cup freshly squeezed lime juice
¼ cup chopped fresh cilantro

Pick over and rinse the beans. Put them into a large bowl and cover completely with cold water. Let the beans soak overnight (or for at least 8 hours). Or use the quicker method described on page 11.

Drain the beans and transfer them to a large pot. Add the 3 cups water. Bring to a boil over medium heat and cook for 5 minutes.

Stir in the onion, garlic, oregano, and bay leaf. Reduce the heat to low and simmer, uncovered, for about 1 hour, until the beans are tender.

Add the chili powder, cumin, coriander, red pepper flakes, and tomato juice, stirring to mix. Continue to cook while preparing the rice.

Put the rice and chicken stock in a medium saucepan. Bring to a boil over medium-high heat. Cover, reduce the heat to low, and simmer for 45 minutes, or until tender.

In the meantime, combine all the salsa ingredients in a small serving bowl and set it aside for the flavors to meld.

When the rice is done, stir it into the bean mixture. Ladle into bowls and serve with the salsa on the side.

Vegetables

*A*rtichokes, *carrots,* cauliflowers, and turnips never used to bring excitement in my life. In fact, I can't remember any vegetable that made my heart sing—until I tasted these favorite vegetable dishes. Of course potatoes are an all-time favorite. And the potato gratin dish—I could make a meal of it!

Oprah

A festive dish of Paella for a dinner party

Sweet Potato Pie with an orange slice garnish on the left,
and Chocolate Tofu Cake on the right

Mixed Greens with Turnips

*R*ed chile pepper and hot sauce add so much punch to this dish that you won't miss the ham or other smoked pork found in the traditional Southern version. I've also added turnips for extra flavor and texture. Stir in the spinach at the last minute, so as not to cook off its inherent nutrients. For variety, Swiss chard leaves can be substituted for the spinach; cook for an additional 3 minutes.

16 cups water
1 cup chopped onion (1 medium onion)
2 garlic cloves, peeled
1 small dried red chile pepper
3 tablespoons white wine or rice wine vinegar
1 bay leaf
1 teaspoon baking soda
3 cups cubed turnip (2 turnips)
5 cups chopped collard greens (1 bunch)
5 cups chopped kale (1 bunch)
5 cups chopped mustard greens (1 large bunch)
4 cups chopped spinach (1 bunch)
3 tablespoons Louisiana-style hot sauce
Freshly ground black pepper to taste

Serves 4

*Fat per serving =
0.9 gram
Calories per serving = 90*

Put the water, onion, garlic, chile pepper, vinegar, and bay leaf in a large pot. Bring to a boil over medium heat. Add the

(continued on page 100)

(Mixed Greens with Turnips, continued)

baking soda, turnips, collard greens, and kale. Bring back to a boil. Reduce the heat to low and simmer, uncovered, for 1 hour.

Add the mustard greens and stir to mix. Cover, raise the heat to medium, and cook for 4 hours.

Just before serving, stir in the spinach, hot sauce, and black pepper.

Taming
Jalapeño Peppers

Most of the heat of jalapeño peppers is contained in the seeds and veins. If you want to tone the kick down a bit, cut the pepper lengthwise, remove the seeds and veins, rinse under cold running water, and finish preparing according to recipe directions.

And remember that the juice of jalapeños and other chile peppers can be rather irritating—wear rubber gloves when handling peppers if you have sensitive skin, and avoid rubbing your eyes.

Roasted Mustard Potatoes

I serve these fiery morsels instead of mashed or baked potatoes. They are so flavorful you can dispense with the usual addition of butter or sour cream.

Light vegetable oil cooking spray
4 tablespoons Dijon-style mustard
2 teaspoons paprika
1 teaspoon ground cumin
1 teaspoon chili powder
⅛ teaspoon cayenne pepper
16 baby red potatoes

Serves 4

*Fat per serving =
1.7 grams
Calories per serving = 137*

Preheat the oven to 400 degrees.

Spray a roasting pan 3 times to coat with the vegetable oil.

Put the mustard, paprika, cumin, chili powder, and cayenne pepper in a large bowl. Whisk to blend. Prick the potatoes several times with the tines of a fork and add them to the bowl. Toss to coat the potatoes evenly. Pour the coated potatoes into the prepared roasting pan, leaving a little space between them.

Bake for about 45 minutes to 1 hour, until the potatoes are fork tender.

Steamed Vegetable Platter

A colorful array of crisp, lightly steamed vegetables, this appetizing side dish can also serve as a hearty meatless meal for two. The pungent, garlicky dressing is anything but bland. Sometimes I garnish with a little minced red bell pepper.

As soon as you top the dish with the cheese, cover it with aluminum foil to trap the heat; this will help melt the cheese by the time you uncover the dish at the table.

Serves 4

Fat per serving = 1.4 grams
Calories per serving = 145

FOR THE DRESSING

6 garlic cloves, peeled and minced
2 teaspoons reduced-sodium soy sauce
2 teaspoons freshly squeezed lemon juice
¼ teaspoon freshly ground black pepper

12 string beans, trimmed
2 medium carrots, trimmed, peeled, and cut
    into ¼-inch rounds
2 cups cauliflower florets
2 ears corn, husked and cut in half
2 small yellow squash, trimmed and cut
    into ¼-inch rounds
2 medium zucchini, trimmed and cut
    into ¼-inch rounds
2 cups broccoli florets

2 teaspoons Spike seasoning
2 slices low-fat cheddar cheese
1 teaspoon freshly grated Parmesan cheese

Put all the dressing ingredients in a small bowl, whisk to blend, and set aside.

Bring water to a boil over high heat in a steamer. Fit the basket into the steamer and put in the string beans, carrots, and cauliflower. Cover and cook for 3 minutes. Add the corn, yellow squash, zucchini, and broccoli. Re-cover and cook for 2 minutes more.

Transfer the vegetables to a warm platter. Arrange the corn around the outer edge of the platter and dust it with the Spike seasoning. Drizzle the dressing over the vegetables in the center and top with the cheddar and Parmesan cheese. Cover briefly with aluminum foil before serving.

Artichokes with Yogurt Mustard

This versatile vegetable can be served as a side dish or an appetizer. For festive presentation, I scoop the yogurt mustard into a hollowed-out red bell pepper and sprinkle a little paprika on top. A few lemon wedges and cherry tomatoes scattered over the artichoke halves add a splash of color. The dish holds up well and can be made hours in advance; just cover and store in the refrigerator.

Serves 4

Fat per serving = 0.3 gram
Calories per serving = 63

½ lemon
6 cups water
4 sprigs fresh parsley
1 bay leaf
5 whole black peppercorns
1 teaspoon dried thyme
2 large artichokes

FOR THE YOGURT MUSTARD

½ cup plain nonfat yogurt
1 teaspoon Dijon-style mustard
⅛ teaspoon lemon pepper
1 teaspoon red wine vinegar
2 tablespoons minced shallot (1 small shallot)

Put the lemon, water, parsley, bay leaf, peppercorns, and thyme in a large pot. Bring to a boil over high heat.

While the water is boiling, prepare the artichokes. Slice ¼ inch off the top of each artichoke. Cut the stems off each, flush with the base, and clip the sharp point at the tip of each leaf with scissors.

Put the artichokes into the boiling water, cover, and cook until the leaves can be pulled from the stem easily, 40 to 50 minutes.

In the meantime, combine all the yogurt-mustard ingredients in a blender and mix at high speed until smooth. Transfer the dressing to a small serving bowl and place it in the center of a large platter.

When the artichokes are done, slice them in half vertically and remove the fuzzy inner chokes. Arrange the artichoke halves cut side down around the yogurt mustard on the platter.

Potato Gratin

A deceptively complex dish that's really quite simple to assemble, this gratin is comprised of layers of thinly sliced potato interspersed with onion rings, zucchini rounds, and spices. I use evaporated skim milk and a little flour to bind and moisten, and to add the richness usually derived from heavy cream.

Serves 8

Fat per serving = 1.9 grams
Calories per serving = 126

Light vegetable oil cooking spray
3 medium baking potatoes, thinly sliced
2 tablespoons all-purpose flour
1 medium onion, trimmed, thinly sliced,
  and separated into rings
⅛ teaspoon cayenne pepper
1 teaspoon paprika
½ teaspoon freshly ground black pepper
2 tablespoons freshly grated Parmesan cheese
1 small zucchini, trimmed and thinly sliced
¼ teaspoon ground nutmeg
½ teaspoon Spike seasoning
12 ounces evaporated skim milk
2 tablespoons chopped fresh parsley

Preheat the oven to 400 degrees.

Coat a 10-inch gratin dish or glass pie plate with 3 sprays of the vegetable oil.

Layer a third of the potatoes over the bottom of the prepared gratin dish or pie plate, overlapping the slices in a spiral pattern. Over the potatoes, sprinkle 1 tablespoon of the flour and arrange the onion rings. Dust with the cayenne pepper and ½ teaspoon of the paprika. Layer another third of the potatoes, adding the remaining tablespoon of flour, the black pepper, and 1 tablespoon of the Parmesan cheese. Scatter the zucchini, dusting with the nutmeg and Spike seasoning. Top with a spiral layer of the remaining potatoes. Pour the evaporated milk over the gratin and add the remaining paprika and Parmesan cheese.

Cover with aluminum foil and bake for 45 minutes. Remove the foil, lower the oven to 350 degrees, and bake for about 15 minutes more, until the top is golden brown. Remove the gratin from the oven and allow it to cool for 10 minutes.

Garnish with the chopped parsley.

Desserts

*W*hether *you're* like me and just want a little something sweet after dinner, or desire a more elaborate treat, these desserts will surely leave you with a sweet smile.

Oprah

Mango Fruit Parfait

This parfait has layers of bright red strawberries, vibrant orange mango puree, pale green kiwi, and deep purplish red raspberries. In the kiwi layer, I position some of the slices upright around the inside of the glass to add texture and detail. For variety, substitute black raspberries or blackberries for the red raspberries on top.

2 cups cubed mango (2 mangoes)
¼ cup freshly squeezed orange juice
24 strawberries, hulled
1 cup peeled and sliced kiwi (4 kiwis)
12 red raspberries

Serves 4

*Fat per serving =
0.8 gram*
Calories per serving = 139

Put the mangoes and orange juice in a blender and puree until smooth.

Slice 20 of the strawberries, leaving 4 whole. Line the bottom of 4 balloon wineglasses with the sliced strawberries. Pour a thin layer of the mango puree over each to cover. Reserving 4 kiwi slices, layer the rest on top of the puree. Divide the remainder of the mango puree among the glasses. Top each with a slice of kiwi surrounded by raspberries. Make a slit in each of the whole strawberries and position 1 on the rim of each glass.

Cover with plastic wrap and refrigerate for 15 minutes.

Sweet Potato Pie

*T*his stylish pie is smooth, rich, creamy—and brimming with spices that conjure up the comforting aromas of holiday baking. In fact, it's a natural replacement for the all too common pumpkin pie. I bake, rather than boil, the sweet potatoes for the filling, which produces a more intense flavor.

On special occasions, I garnish each serving of the pie with a dollop of mock whipped cream and a sprinkle of ground nutmeg or cinnamon.

Serves 12

Fat per serving = 3.8 grams
Calories per serving = 141

FOR THE CRUST

Light vegetable oil cooking spray
2 cups graham cracker crumbs
2 teaspoons ground cinnamon
1 large egg white

FOR THE FILLING

4 baked medium sweet potatoes (see Box, opposite)
6 large egg whites
¼ teaspoon ground nutmeg
¼ teaspoon ground cloves
¼ teaspoon ground allspice
¼ teaspoon ground ginger
2 tablespoons pure vanilla extract
5 tablespoons pure maple syrup

1 tablespoon honey
6 ounces light cream cheese
¼ cup freshly squeezed orange juice

Preheat the oven to 350 degrees.

Spray a 10-inch round pie pan 3 times with the vegetable oil to coat.

Put all the remaining ingredients for the crust in the bowl of a food processor. Pulse 5 times. Transfer the mixture to the prepared pan and press down firmly, spreading the crumb crust until it covers the bottom evenly.

Peel the sweet potatoes, then put them in a large mixing bowl and mash them with a fork. Transfer the potatoes to a blender and add all the remaining filling ingredients. Whip until the mixture is smooth and frothy, scraping down the sides as necessary so all the ingredients are blended. Pour the filling into the crust.

Bake for 30 to 45 minutes, until the center of the pie is firm and not sticky to the touch. Transfer the pan to a rack and allow the pie to cool for 30 minutes, then refrigerate for 1 hour.

Baking Sweet Potatoes

Preheat the oven to 350 degrees.

Scrub and dry the sweet potatoes. Prick the surface of each potato 4 times with the tines of a fork. Place the potatoes onto the center rack of the oven and bake for about 1 hour, until tender.

Chocolate Tofu Cake

My version of chocolate cheesecake provides all of the treat with none of the guilt. I've replaced the typical bulk ration of cream cheese with tofu, using just enough light cream cheese and ricotta cheese to flavor and add texture. Unsweetened cocoa powder replaces baking chocolate, while honey sweetens the mix instead of sugar. A thin white topping contrasts dramatically with the deep chocolate hue of the cake.

For a striking finish, decorate the top with a chocolate sauce design.

Serves 12

Fat per serving =
3.9 grams
Calories per serving = 92

Light vegetable oil cooking spray
8 ounces firm tofu
¼ cup part skim milk ricotta cheese
4 ounces light cream cheese
¼ cup pure maple syrup
3 tablespoons unsweetened cocoa powder
2 large egg whites
1 tablespoon ground cinnamon
3 tablespoons light Irish cream liqueur
1 tablespoon coffee liqueur

FOR THE TOPPING

½ cup nonfat sour cream or plain nonfat yogurt
1 teaspoon pure vanilla extract
1 tablespoon honey

Preheat the oven to 350 degrees.

Coat a 10-inch glass pie plate with 3 sprays of the vegetable oil.

In the bowl of a food processor, combine the tofu, ricotta cheese, cream cheese, maple syrup, cocoa powder, egg whites, cinnamon, and the liqueurs. Puree until smooth and pour into the prepared pie plate.

Place the pie plate on the center rack of the oven. On the bottom rack, place a baking pan filled halfway with water. Bake for 1 hour.

While the cake is baking, combine all the topping ingredients in a small bowl and whisk thoroughly.

When the cake has cooked for an hour, remove it from the oven, spread the topping on evenly, decorate if you wish, and return it to the oven. Bake for about 10 minutes more, until the topping sets.

Refrigerate for 2 hours before serving. Decorate with the Chocolate Sauce Design, page 116, if you wish

Making
Mock Whipped Cream

Put a can of evaporated skim milk in the refrigerator and a stainless steel bowl and the beaters from an electric mixer into the freezer for an hour. Put the milk into the chilled bowl, add 1 teaspoon each of pure vanilla extract and of brandy, and beat at high speed just until peaks are formed. Use immediately.

Making a Chocolate Sauce Design

Put a mixture of 2 tablespoons pure maple syrup and 2 tablespoons unsweetened cocoa powder into a squeeze bottle or an improvised pastry bag, which can be made by forcing the sauce into a bottom corner of a sturdy plastic storage bag and pricking a small hole through which it can flow. Squeeze a series of straight lines across the cake, then rake the tines of a fork across the top in the opposite direction to create a pattern.

Peach Crepes

This sophisticated dessert is light and refreshing. Making crepes is fairly easy, as long as you allow yourself a little leeway for initial trial and error. Don't be disappointed if your first crepe or two aren't perfect, as the pan needs to be seasoned and to reach just the right heat. Although the recipe yields 8 crepes, there's enough batter for 12 to 14.

For a really elegant presentation, top each crepe with a crystallized violet and scatter a few blueberries around.

FOR THE CREPES

½ cup all-purpose flour
1 large egg
3 tablespoons Amaretto-flavored nondairy creamer
½ cup skim milk
⅛ teaspoon ground nutmeg
1 teaspoon pure vanilla extract
Light vegetable oil cooking spray

FOR THE FILLING

2 cups freshly squeezed orange juice
2 tablespoons orange liqueur
8 peaches, peeled and thinly sliced

(continued on page 118)

Serves 8

*Fat per serving =
1.5 grams
Calories per serving = 125*

(Peach Crepes, continued)

1 teaspoon honey
1 teaspoon ground cinnamon
1 teaspoon orange zest

Put the flour into a mixing bowl. Make a well in the center of the flour and add the egg. While whisking, pour in the nondairy creamer and then the skim milk. Continue to whisk until the batter is smooth and free of lumps, then whisk in the nutmeg and vanilla. Cover the batter and set it aside for 30 minutes.

Preheat an 8-inch nonstick crepe pan or a small, heavy nonstick frying pan for about 1 minute over medium-high heat. Spray it twice with the vegetable oil. Spoon just enough batter into the pan to form a thin layer over the bottom, about 3 tablespoons, and tilt the pan to spread the batter evenly. Cook the crepe for 1 to 2 minutes, just until the edge is firm and begins to separate from the bottom. Flip the crepe with a spatula and cook for 1 to 2 minutes more on the other side, until golden brown. Remove the crepe to a sheet of waxed paper. Continue the process, stacking the cooked crepes on the waxed paper, until 8 crepes have been made.

For the filling, combine the orange juice, liqueur, peaches, and honey in a medium frying pan. Cook for about 10 minutes, until the liquid turns thick and syrupy.

To assemble, lay a crepe on an individual serving plate. Mound ⅓ cup of the peach slices on the bottom half of each and flip the top half over. Spoon a tablespoon of the peach syrup over each and dust with cinnamon and orange zest.

Fruit Kebabs

This is an appetizing way to serve fruit—one that will appeal to youngsters as well as to adults. I like to serve fruit kebabs garnished with lime wedges at breakfast, along with spiced bran muffins right out of the oven. They also make great snacks or a healthy dessert.

Eight 12-inch wooden skewers
1½ cups fresh pineapple cubes
Eight ½-inch kiwi slices (2 kiwis)
2 cups cubed papaya (1 papaya)
2 cups cubed watermelon
16 strawberries, hulled

Thread an assortment of fruit on each skewer with a strawberry at either end. Serve chilled.

Spiced Bran Muffins

I know that bran is an important source of carbohydrates and fiber, but the primary appeal of these muffins is their flavor. They taste a little like gingerbread, only with raisins and nuts. The muffins are great with apple butter and with fruit kebabs alongside (see Box, page 119).

Makes 12 muffins

Fat per muffin =
2.1 grams
Calories per muffin = 123

Light vegetable oil cooking spray
½ cup molasses
2 tablespoons honey
2 large egg whites
¼ cup plain nonfat yogurt
¼ cup 2% milk
½ cup wheat bran
1 cup whole wheat flour
1½ teaspoons baking powder
1 tablespoon ground ginger
1 teaspoon ground cloves
¼ cup chopped walnuts
¼ cup golden raisins

Preheat the oven to 350 degrees.

Coat a 12-well muffin tin with the cooking spray.

Warm the molasses and honey in a small saucepan over low heat just until it begins to steam. Remove the pan from the heat and set it aside to cool.

Whisk the egg whites, yogurt, and milk together in a large mixing bowl until blended. Whisk in the molasses-and-honey mixture. Using a wooden spoon, stir in the bran, flour, baking powder, and spices. Fold in the walnuts and raisins.

Turn the batter into the prepared muffin tin and bake for 15 to 20 minutes, until a tester inserted into the center of a muffin comes out clean. Serve warm.

Oatmeal Muffins

*T*his far from ordinary oatmeal muffin incorporates an intriguing mix of tastes and textures—including orange juice and zest, lots of spices, zesty dried cranberries, and crunchy pecans. Be sure to use rolled oats, not the quick-cooking variety.

The recipe is easily converted to mini muffins for the perfect midday snack in lieu of cookies. Simply pour the batter into a prepared 24-well mini muffin tin and bake for about 12 minutes.

Makes 12 muffins

Fat per muffin =
2.5 grams
Calories per muffin = 128

Light vegetable oil cooking spray
2 large egg whites
⅓ cup pure maple syrup
3 tablespoons freshly squeezed orange juice
1 cup skim milk
1 tablespoon pure vanilla extract
1 teaspoon ground cinnamon
⅛ teaspoon ground allspice
⅛ teaspoon ground cloves
⅛ teaspoon ground nutmeg
1 tablespoon orange zest
1½ cups rolled oats
1 cup whole wheat flour

1 teaspoon baking powder
¼ cup chopped pecans
¼ cup dried cranberries

Preheat the oven to 350 degrees.

Spray a 12-well muffin tin 3 times with the vegetable oil.

Put the egg whites in a large mixing bowl and whisk until frothy. Whisk in the maple syrup, orange juice, and milk. Add the vanilla, cinnamon, allspice, cloves, nutmeg, and orange zest. Whisk to blend. Stir in the oats, flour, and baking powder with a wooden spoon. Fold in the pecans and dried cranberries.

Fill the muffin tin with the batter (each cup should be approximately two-thirds full). Bake for about 20 minutes, until the muffins are firm in the center.

If you do not find in your supermarket any of the following seasonings that I call for in my recipes, you can ask the store manager to order them or write or phone the manufacturers yourself to place an order:

Spike seasoning
Modern Products Inc.
Gayelord Hauser Product
3015 West Vera Avenue
Milwaukee, WI 53209
1-800-877-8935

Creole or Cajun seasoning
Creole Foods
P.O. Box 1687
Opeloussas, LA 70571
1-800-551-9066

Old Bay Seasoning
Old Bay Seasoning Company–Consumer Affairs
211 Schilling Circle
Hunt Valley, MD 21031
1-800-632-5847

Index

crabcakes, un-fried, 45–6
cream of broccoli soup,
     14–15
crepes, peach, 117–18
curries, 36
     chicken salad, 34–5
     mushroom soup, 18–19

desserts, 109–23
     chocolate tofu cake,
          114–15
     fruit
          kebabs, 119
          mango parfait, 111
          peach crepes, 117–18
     muffins
          oatmeal, 122–3
          spiced bran, 120–1
     sweet potato pie,
          112–13
duck
     breast of, roasted, with
          pineapple chutney,
          92–3
     choosing Muscovy, 91

eggplant
     in grilled vegetable sand-
          wich, 75–7

eggplant *(continued)*
     in mixed vegetable pizza
          with blue cheese,
          70–1
entrees, 79–95
     chicken, roast, with seed
          bread stuffing, 83–5
     duck breast, roasted, with
          pineapple chutney,
          92–3
     paella, 81–2
     peppered tuna Niçoise,
          86–7
     red beans and rice with
          salsa, 94–5
     shrimp, skewered, on wild
          rice pilaf, 88–90
evaporated skim milk,
     low-fat, 14

French fries, un-fried, 44
fruit, 4
     kebabs, 119
     mango parfait, 111
     peach crepes, 117–18

garlic
     angel hair with lemon
          and, 58–9

garlic *(continued)*
     in pesto, 57
garnishes, 3
     carrot flowers, 17
     fresh herb, 5
     kale, purple, flowering, 83
     orange wheels, 31
     radish rosettes, 26
     scallion starbursts, 53
     value of, 3
ginger chicken, spinach
          fettucini with, 54–6
goat cheese pizza with
          artichokes and onion,
          68
greens, mixed, with turnips,
          99–100
grilling, stovetop, 27

herbs, fresh, 4–5

ingredients, low-fat, 4–5

jalapeño peppers, 100

kale, purple, flowering, as a
          garnish, 83
kebabs, fruit, 117–18

techniques, 4–5

tomato(es)
  salad, bruschetta with, 72–3
  sauce, fresh, pesto linguine in, 52–3
  sun-dried
    mixed vegetable pizza with blue cheese and, 70–1
    penne with chicken and, 49–51

tuna Niçoise, peppered, 86–7

turnips, mixed greens with, 99–100

un-fried foods, 37–46
  catfish, 42–3

un-fried foods *(continued)*
  chicken, 39–40
  crabcakes, 45–6
  French fries, 44

vegetable(s), 4, 97–107
  artichokes with yogurt mustard, 104–5
  barley stew, with lentils, 16–17
  mixed greens with turnips, 99–100
  pizza, with blue cheese, 70–1
  potatoes
    gratin, 106–7
    roasted mustard, 101
    un-fried French fries, 44
  purees in soups, 4

vegetable(s) *(continued)*
  sandwich, grilled, 75–7
  steamed, platter, 102–3

vinegars, 5
  white balsamic, 5

whipped cream, mock, 116

yogurt, 5
  mustard, 104–5

zucchini
  in grilled vegetable sandwich, 75–7
  in mixed vegetable pizza with blue cheese, 70–1
  in steamed vegetable platter, 102–3

A NOTE ON THE TYPE

The text of this book was set on the Macintosh in a digitized version of Garamond, a rendering of the type first cut by Claude Garamond (c. 1480–1561). Garamond was a pupil of Geoffrey Tory and is believed to have based his letters on the Venetian models, although he introduced a number of important differences, and it is to him we owe the letter which we know as "old style." He gave to his letters a certain elegance and a feeling of movement that won for their creator an immediate reputation and the patronage of Francis I of France.

Printed and bound by Arcata Graphics/Martinsburg,
Martinsburg, West Virginia
Rose ornament by Karin Kretschmann
Design by Virginia Tan